MEASURING ORGANIZATIONAL IMPROVEMENT IMPACT

A Practical Guide To Successfully Linking
Organizational Improvement Measures

Richard Y. Chang
Paul De Young

Richard Chang Associates, Inc.
Publications Division
Irvine, California

MEASURING ORGANIZATIONAL IMPROVEMENT IMPACT

A Practical Guide To Successfully Linking
Organizational Improvement Measures

Richard Y. Chang
Paul De Young

Library of Congress Catalog Card Number
95-92579

ISBN 1-883553-17-2

Second printing May 1996

Richard Chang Associates, Inc.
Publications Division
41 Corporate Park, Suite 230
Irvine, CA 92714
(800) 756-8096 • Fax (714) 756-0853

ACKNOWLEDGMENTS

About The Authors

Richard Y. Chang is President and CEO of Richard Chang Associates, Inc., a diversified organizational improvement consulting and publishing firm based in Irvine, California. He is internationally recognized for his management strategy, quality improvement, organization development, customer satisfaction, and human resource development expertise.

Paul De Young is an Organizational Development Specialist at Children's Hospital of Orange County. His extensive background and areas of research include organizational measurement, organizational culture and change, total quality management, and productivity gain sharing. Paul is also an Affiliate Professor of Industrial/Organizational Psychology at United States International University, and a former consultant of Richard Chang Associates, Inc.

The authors would like to acknowledge the support of the entire team of professionals at Richard Chang Associates, Inc. for their contribution to the guidebook development process. In addition, special thanks are extended to the many client organizations who have helped to shape the practical ideas and proven methods shared in this guidebook.

Additional Credits

Editor:	Ruth Stingley
Reviewer:	Keith Kelly
Graphic Layout:	Christina Slater
Cover Design:	John Odam Design Associates

PREFACE

The 1990's have already presented individuals and organizations with some very difficult challenges to face and overcome. So who will have the advantage as we move toward the year 2000 and beyond?

The advantage will belong to those with a commitment to continuous learning. Whether on an individual basis or as an entire organization, one key ingredient to building a continuous learning environment is *The Practical Guidebook Collection* brought to you by the Publications Division of Richard Chang Associates, Inc.

After understanding the future *"learning needs"* expressed by our clients and other potential customers, we are pleased to publish *The Practical Guidebook Collection*. These guidebooks are designed to provide you with proven, *"real-world"* tips, tools, and techniques— on a wide range of subjects—that you can apply in the workplace and/or on a personal level immediately.

Once you've had a chance to benefit from *The Practical Guidebook Collection*, please share your feedback with us. We've included a brief *Evaluation and Feedback Form* at the end of the guidebook that you can fax to us at (714) 756-0853.

With your feedback, we can continuously improve the resources we are providing through the Publications Division of Richard Chang Associates, Inc.

Wishing you successful reading,

Richard Y. Chang
President and CEO
Richard Chang Associates, Inc.

TABLE OF CONTENTS

"What's the use of running fast if you're not on the right road?"

Old German Proverb

CHAPTER ONE

INTRODUCTION

Why Read This Guidebook?

Improvement is a relative term. It is defined by a starting point, a desired goal, and a process of tracking progress from start to finish. As individuals, we learn to build measurement into our improvement efforts from an early age. Our parents and our schools provide us with the measures, the feedback, and the incentives to improve our grades, our athletic endeavors, and even our day-to-day participation in household activities. We thus learn a personal improvement methodology that best fits us as unique individuals and reflects the environment in which we operate.

Isn't organizational improvement important as well? And what about measuring improvement? What method for measuring improvement works best in an organizational setting? This guidebook will help answer these questions. It provides a systematic measurement methodology that is complete, and yet at the same time is flexible enough to accommodate the needs of a wide variety of sizes and types of organizations.

If your organization or work group is serious about getting better at what it does, then measuring improvement is critical to your success. The following chapters offer a proven model for measuring organizational performance improvement starting with the *"big-picture"* organizational result areas and their related measures. These measures are then cascaded down through the alignment of work group measures and improvement efforts linked to the *"big picture."*

Who Should Read This Guidebook?

Managers, supervisors, team leaders, and work group members in all parts of the organization will be able to use this guidebook to help design their groups' measurement and improvement processes.

If you are on a process improvement team, you'll find this guidebook a valuable tool to help select measures and targets for your improvement efforts.

Process improvement coaches, facilitators, and external consultants will be able to draw from the measurement model to help guide the design and implementation of improvement efforts that track back to organizational targets.

Whatever your position or title, if your involvement in organizational improvement provides you with the opportunity to measure your progress, then this guidebook is for you. It will help you establish the right measures, and determine how to track information to gauge your success against these measures.

When And How To Use It

Use the guidebook at planning meetings, training sessions, and in small group or team sessions when people are focusing on what work is done, how it is done, and how the improvements are measured. Refer to it often, and use it to help build a framework to guide the direction of your organizational improvement efforts.

❑ While Getting Started...

Use this guidebook at the beginning of any organizational or work group effort as you design your improvement plan. It will help you incorporate a strong sense of direction and clarity into your improvement initiatives. The use of a measurement process will crystallize the plan, turning it into a meaningful and measurable set of outcomes that everyone will be able to understand, relate to, and most importantly—contribute to.

❏ During Ongoing Implementation…

If you already have an improvement initiative underway, then use this guidebook to help revitalize your efforts and, if necessary, to strengthen the element of measurement.

Organizational improvement often brings with it organizational change, which can lead to uncertainty and even resistance among people involved. By clarifying the improvement plan through the eight-step measurement model in the guidebook, you'll find that people will be much more likely to understand where things are going and will be better able to plan for their role and contribution to the process.

So, don't hesitate to use the methodology in this guidebook part way into the race to help keep the *"fuel"* pumping through the organizational improvement engine.

❏ As Outcomes Are Achieved…

Although there really should never be an end to an organization's efforts to improve itself and better meet the needs of its customers, you'll find that this guidebook provides valuable insights into measuring actual outcomes against a work group or organization's targets.

In addition, you can use this guidebook as a tool for analyzing how and why you obtained your results at the end of the quarter, year, or other period chosen as the time in which certain targets are to be reached.

However you decide to use the measurement methodology, feel free to adapt it to your specific needs. And don't forget to photocopy and use the reproducible forms and tools in the Appendix.

A QUICK LOOK AT MEASUREMENT

Why Measure?

In our complex and competitive business world, we must continually improve the quality and productivity of our products and services to stay ahead of the competition. Yet, organizations can effectively improve only that which they can effectively measure. To improve continually then, we need a method to help us understand where we are now, to help us plan where we want to go, and to tell us when we have arrived.

At Children's Hospital...

Richard Garcia runs the Environmental Services Department. He wants to improve his department's impact on customer satisfaction because the hospital's administration reports that they have too many complaints. Richard directs his employees to work harder and more efficiently, but he has no evidence of any increase in customer satisfaction. In fact, his employees feel that they are already working as hard as they can.

Subsequently, Richard starts tracking where complaints are coming from and their frequency. He and his staff learn where and when problems most frequently occur. Richard can prevent complaints from happening in the first place by eliminating the root cause of the biggest problem areas. He does; and, as a result, customer complaints are down and satisfaction has increased.

Woolf Software Company has a vision...

that they will be the *"premier infotainment software producer in the world by the year 2000."* They define their measurement system by the following result areas: market share, new product development, and customer satisfaction. Each of these result areas has a unique set of indicators *(or measures)* that help determine success for each corresponding result area.

As you can see from these examples, measurement is an important ingredient in the organizational recipe for success. Following are three very important reasons why you should measure your improvement efforts.

Reason #1: To Provide Focus, Direction, And A Common Understanding

Most managers would agree that leading their employees to improve their operating practices is difficult if it is not clear where to go. Vision and mission statements do a good job of providing overall guidance and direction. However, good measures provide the operational definitions everybody can clearly understand.

Reason #2: To Provide Knowledge For Making Better Decisions

Good data helps managers and employees make good decisions. The more you understand how your processes perform, the better you can figure out how to improve them. Processes should only be improved when they are relatively stable. Otherwise, you may be tampering with the process, which can cause more harm than good.

Gus, a plant manager for more than twenty-two years, uses his *"gut instinct"* when deciding how many parts to order for the assembly plant. He estimates the right number of parts most of the time and does this based on his experience from last year's sales. Unfortunately, this year's sales are erratic and unpredictable. This has often resulted in either too many or too few parts ordered for the assembly line.

Such decisions, based only on *"gut-level"* instincts without true knowledge from process data, often results in an upset stomach. A prescription for success requires decisions based on knowledge from reliable data.

Reason #3: To Provide Feedback On Organizational Improvement Efforts

How will you know if your organizational improvement efforts are successful without data to back them up? Can you imagine dieting without having any way of knowing you have lost weight? Organizational improvement requires ongoing feedback to tell you where you are now and how much farther you have to go.

"Your guess is as good as mine."

Features Of Excellent Measurement Systems

"Data, data, everywhere, and none to help you think."

Admittedly a bad pun from Samuel Taylor Coleridge's famous line, it is unfortunately true that most of us in organizations are surrounded by data that we cannot use. Many leaders find themselves data rich and information poor (*DRIPs*).

The challenge for most leaders is to examine all their data and reports and weed out the inappropriate measures from the appropriate ones. The following are guidelines and considerations for establishing an effective measurement system.

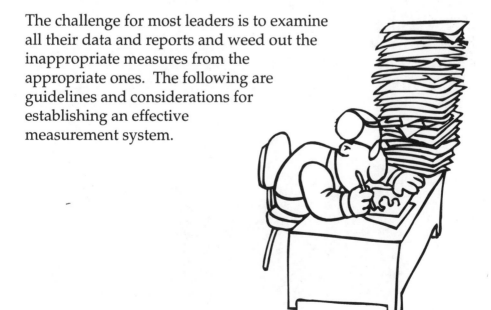

1. A system should provide information-rich data which is "actionable."

Some systems generate loads of excess measurement detail and paperwork that is essentially useless to those analyzing the data. Reports that contain excessive data detail over long periods of time (*or on too frequent a basis*) are too complicated for executives, managers, and employees trying to observe and act on trends. *"Visual"* trend charts would be much more appropriate.

2. A system should contain a masterful blend of both efficiency and effectiveness indicators.

Some systems focus primarily on efficiency-oriented indicators while others are overly concerned with effectiveness-focused indicators. A good system should contain useful measures in both realms. For example, an average time for preparing member statements may be important for analyzing work group productivity, but the average number of complaints for incomplete statements would also be valuable to scrutinize the quality of the work being performed.

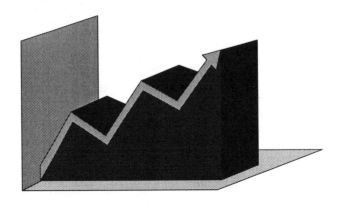

3. A system should include measures that focus on accomplishment, reward-oriented categories.

Many systems focus primarily on negative measurement categories, such as error rates, failure rates, trouble report rates, complaints per hour, etc. While these measures are important, a system should also include categories that can demonstrate successes, such as percent of commitments met, number of appointments met on time, percent of customers satisfied with service, etc.

4. Don't measure A and hope for B.

An improved measure in one area doesn't always mean improvements in a seemingly related area. For example, measuring the time a service representative spends on the phone with a customer doesn't necessarily serve as a measure of improved customer service.

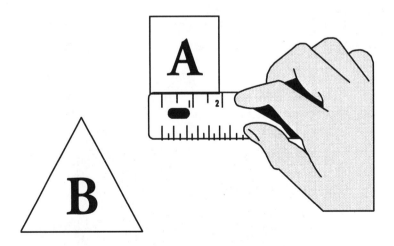

5. Measures should be easy to understand.

Technical terms and industry jargon are appropriate for those who understand them, but not everyone in the organization will. Therefore, the reviewing audience should be carefully considered. For example, technically-oriented reports on computer mainframe performance may be difficult for a Customer Service Process Improvement Team to decipher.

6. Managers or employees should be accountable for measurement accuracy and results.

Theoretically, measurement systems and methods are best managed and tracked by those who are closest to the items being measured. Nevertheless, factors such as incentive plans linked to productivity or quality, a general *"halo effect"* of a work group's performance, or avoidance of accountability can all affect measurement categories, as well as the accuracy and results of the data in those categories.

7. A work group should only be accountable for measures over which they have control.

Some systems inappropriately hold work groups responsible for categories of measurement they cannot influence. A customer service work group, for example, isn't necessarily accountable for an increase in customer complaints related to incomplete orders being received by the customer.

8. Measurement information should be analyzed and acted upon in a timely manner.

A measurement system may provide data in a concise, understandable, timely manner, yet those who analyze the information need to do so quickly and decisively. Data which indicates alarming trends, such as rapidly increasing problems with product inventory or customer service levels, should be scrutinized immediately by the appropriate parties, regardless of regularly scheduled periods of analysis.

9. Measures should be cost-effective to collect.

The value of the data to be gathered should be weighed against the cost of gathering, collating, summarizing, and distributing the information. If it costs many thousands of dollars to manage the measures surrounding inter-office mail distribution, then the potential cost-benefit payoff should be analyzed carefully.

10. A measurement system should focus on continuous improvement, rather than just compliance and control.

While standards and requirements are clearly important, a system should also encourage measures and analyses that facilitate continuous improvement. If, for example, order processing times are exceeding acceptable control levels, and employees are complaining about inferior work processes and tools, it may be worthwhile to measure the number of process improvement ideas generated per week via suggestion systems or improvement teams as well.

Continuous Improvement

CHAPTER TWO WORKSHEET:
WHY MEASURE IMPROVEMENT EFFORTS?

Examining why you might want to engage in *"measurable"* organizational improvement is important. Please respond to the following questions:

1. What are some anticipated changes and challenges faced in your industry in the next three to five years?

_____

_____

_____

_____

_____

2. Considering your current knowledge of organizational improvement, how might a measurement system help address the challenges discussed in #1 above?

_____

_____

_____

_____

_____

3. What personal benefits do you anticipate experiencing from your involvement in developing a measurement system?

_____

_____

_____

_____

_____

_____

_____

_____

4. What key organizational benefits do you anticipate from implementing a measurement system?

_____

_____

_____

_____

_____

_____

_____

_____

MEASUREMENT IN ACTION

Let's face it—measuring things is not like eating ice cream. It takes both creativity and hard work. However, an organization-wide measurement system has tremendous value when good data provides good information to help leaders make sound business decisions to drive their improvement efforts. An organization can develop a measurement system in several ways. The following is an overview of one way that will guide you, along the path of developing an effective measurement system.

A Case Example: Western Books, Inc.

Western Books, Inc....

is a wholesale book distribution company. They distribute management and business-related books to retailers throughout the United States. Since the founding of the company ten years ago, the executive team has spent three days each year at an offsite conference. There they work on revising their strategic plan and developing new goals and tactical plans. Yet their business remains flat, despite everyone's desire to increase market share, revenue, and profits, as outlined in the strategic plan.

Most managers agree that the problem is that once they write the strategic plan, polish it, and publish it in an attractive four-color brochure, it usually finds its way to their bookshelves—not to be looked at again until the next strategic planning session. Michelle Stames, Chief Training Officer, privately says that their strategic plan has a *"great shelf life, but no real life."*

Michelle recently returned from a conference on improving organizational performance where she heard about a simple, step-by-step model for developing an organization-wide measurement system. She knew immediately that this could help Western Books achieve its strategic goals. However, Michelle must persuade the executive team to adopt this model and help implement it throughout their organization....

The Measurement Linkage Model

The following Measurement Linkage Model™ is designed to help a work group start a measurement system in their area. An organization should link all work group measurement systems to one organization-wide system where organization-wide Key Result Areas (KRAs) and Key Indicators (KIs) cascade down throughout the organization.

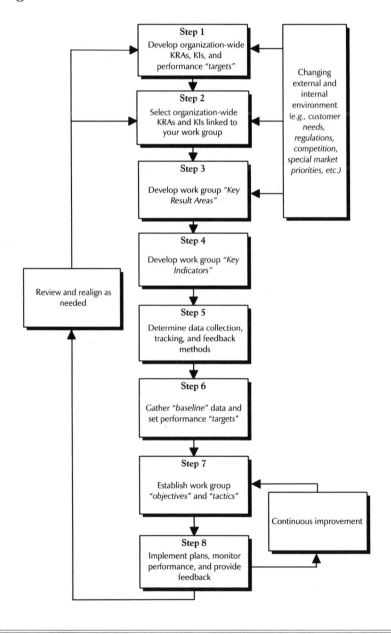

Developing A Measurement System

Developing a measurement system that works for your organization requires planning. The eight steps take you through the planning to the implementation of a successful measurement system. Become acquainted with the steps. They could prove valuable to both you and your organization.

| Step 1 |
| Develop organization-wide |
| KRAs, KIs, and |
| performance "targets" |

Step One: Develop Organization-Wide KRAs, KIs And Performance "Targets"

♦ An organization's vision, mission, and strategic plan provide direction for work groups throughout the organization.

♦ An executive team must first develop KRAs, KIs and performance "*targets*" to quantify its strategic plan into measurable components.

♦ Managers and all employees should have a clear understanding of this information to develop a measurement system that assesses improvement impact for their work group.

Michelle met with the executive team...

to propose that they develop an *"organization-wide"* measurement system first, and then pilot a work group measurement system in the Order Fulfillment Department. She started by describing the first step toward developing a measurement system.

One of the executive team members asked for a better definition of a KRA, a KI, and a performance target. Michelle provided the following definition:

"Key Result Areas (KRAs) are critical, 'must achieve,' 'make-or-break' performance categories for an organization. A Key Indicator (KI) is a specific measure which helps determine how well you are performing in a given KRA. Therefore, KRAs focus on an organization's outputs." Michelle paused for a moment, then continued describing step one and the rest of the steps, using overhead transparencies to highlight each of them....

An organization may have as few as four or as many as ten Key Result Areas, depending on the complexity of its environment, industry, and customer composition. An example of a KRA category is customer loyalty. Customer loyalty, then, contains several Key Indicators (*e.g., customer satisfaction ratings, customer retention, customer complaint resolution, etc.*).

A KI operationally defines a KRA. A KI is the metric or yardstick by which an organization can evaluate achievement toward its KRAs. For example, let's say one KRA is health and fitness. For that KRA the KIs include: percent of body fat, blood pressure, cholesterol levels, heart rate at rest and on a treadmill, etc. You get the point.

Performance targets, then, turn the KIs into tangible goals. These targets help set the *"gauges"* that will determine organization-wide progress and provide measurable feedback on efforts towards the KRAs. Examples of specific performance targets include:

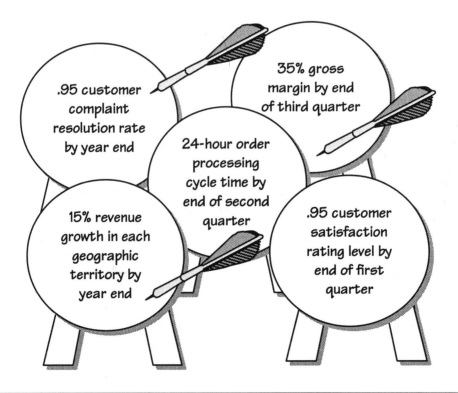

.95 customer complaint resolution rate by year end

35% gross margin by end of third quarter

24-hour order processing cycle time by end of second quarter

15% revenue growth in each geographic territory by year end

.95 customer satisfaction rating level by end of first quarter

Step 2

Select organization-wide
KRAs and KIs linked to
your work group

Step Two: Select Organization-Wide KRAs And KIs Linked To Your Work Group

◆ All work groups produce products and/or services in support of the organization's goals.

◆ Work groups select the appropriate organization-wide KRAs and KIs to which they directly contribute.

Note: Not all organization-wide KRAs and KIs are necessarily related to an individual work group's outputs.

Step 3

Develop work group
"Key Result Areas"

Step Three: Develop Work Group "Key Result Areas"

◆ Work groups categorize primary product or service outputs provided to their customer(s).

◆ They identify categories of work-group specific KRAs which may be in addition to the specific linked KRAs selected in Step 2.

◆ They examine *"the big picture"* of their work group as a system of suppliers, inputs, processes, outputs, customers and customer requirements.

◆ Good KRAs answer the question, *"Which are the most critical work group performance outcomes we must achieve?"*

Step 4
Develop work group *"Key Indicators"*

Step Four: Develop Work Group "Key Indicators"

- KIs break each KRA into measurable components.

- KIs are the *"yardsticks"* by which one can measure progress.

- Develop two to four KIs for each work-group specific KRA established in Step 3.

- It takes time to establish the right KIs. Once established, they will be used to track trends.

- Good KIs answer the question, *"How will a work group know if it is making progress toward its KRAs?"*

Step 5
Determine data collection, tracking, and feedback methods

Step Five: Determine Data Collection, Tracking, And Feedback Methods

- Methods for KI data collection and feedback are critical in determining the success of the work group's measurement system.

- This step determines how, where, and when data will be collected.

- Determine who is accountable for monitoring, reporting, and using the results to make decisions.

Step 6
Gather *"baseline"* data and set performance *"targets"*

Step Six: Gather "Baseline" Data And Set Performance "Targets"

- *"Baseline"* data provides an excellent source of information to help identify performance levels *(or "targets")*.

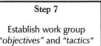

Step 7

Establish work group
"objectives" and *"tactics"*

Step Seven: Establish Work Group "Objectives" And "Tactics"

- ◆ Work groups identify improvement opportunities and make plans for action.

- ◆ This is the *"road map"* to help achieve the *"targets."*

- ◆ Once a work group makes improvement plans, they need to take specific action to improve performance.

TACTICS

OBJECTIVES

Step 8
Implement plans,
monitor performance,
and provide feedback

Step Eight: Implement Plans, Monitor Performance, And Provide Feedback

- ◆ Continually monitor performance of the work group.

- ◆ Provide feedback to appropriate managers/employees so they can continue to improve the work group.

- ◆ Monitor the measurement system to ensure the work group is continuing to measure the right things.

- ◆ Adjust the measurement system as the business shifts its focus and responds to an ever-changing world.

Michelle was successful...

in clearly presenting her ideas using the overhead transparencies. However, the executive team wasn't convinced they needed to modify their current way of measuring things. Walter Graham, Chief Financial Officer, commented with, *"I have no need to modify the measurement system since my department has all the data we could possibly handle."*

Lynda Gayle-Williams, Manager of the Order Fulfillment Department, responded that her department also had plenty of data that was financial in nature, but she knew nothing about the quality of their services, satisfaction of customers, performance of their processes, and the satisfaction of her staff.

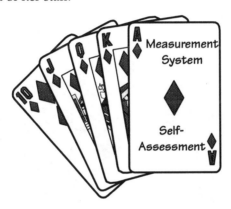

Michelle had another ace...

up her sleeve. At the same conference where she heard about this measurement system methodology, she received a measurement system self-assessment. Michelle distributed copies of the questionnaire to the executive team and said that if they scored high enough on the measurement audit, she would drop the entire issue. She added, *"However, if you do not score well, the executive team must agree to seriously examine the organization's measurement system and 'reengineer' if necessary."* The executive team agreed. Michelle administered the assessment on the following page....

Assessing Your Current Measurement Efforts

To improve your measurement efforts, assessing where you currently stand will be helpful. The following self-assessment will provide you valuable input with regards to how your organization's approach to measurement *"measures up!"*

Measurement System Self-Assessment

Rating Scale: Read each of the following statements. For each statement, rate our current measurement system based on the following response scale:

5 = Strongly Agree   4 = Agree   3 = Neither Agree Nor Disagree
2 = Disagree   1 = Strongly Disagree

__2__   1. Our current measurement system measures all the right things.

__4__   2. We collect measures linked to organizational improvement goals.

__2__   3. We define our measures from the customers' *"point of view."*

__4__   4. Our measurement system does not focus solely on *"bottom-line"* financial results.

__1__   5. This organization uses measurement data to promote continuous improvement and learning.

__1__   6. Our measurement system does not generate more paperwork than is necessary.

__1__   7. Our measurement system always gives us the information we need when we need it.

__2__   8. Our measurement system focuses on continuous improvement rather than compliance and control.

__2__   9. We are only accountable for measures for which we have control.

__3__   10. Our measures focus on the *"positive"* side rather than the *"negative"* side *(e.g., appointments met versus appointments missed).*

__2__   11. Our measurement system contains both objective and subjective measures.

__1__   12. Everyone understands the measures used to evaluate performance.

__3__   13. Managers or employees are accountable for measurement accuracy and results.

__3__   14. We act on measurement results quickly.

__2__   15. All data collection methods are cost-effective.

2   16. We always communicate measurement results to the appropriate managers and employees.

4   17. Our measures focus on effectiveness (*e.g., number of on-time arrivals*) and efficiency (*e.g., response time*).

2   18. All measures are reliable.

1   19. Senior leadership built our measurement system with a plan. It did not evolve by chance.

3   20. Measures show change when we make improvement efforts.

2   21. We have a method for screening out measures that we really do not use.

3   22. Our measurement system contains a *"well-balanced"* blend of KRAs reflecting our mission, vision, and strategic goals.

3   23. Our measurement system provides information that allows us to set clear objectives.

2   24. Objectives are based on a clear understanding of the performance capability of our systems and processes.

2   25. Important work that crosses functions gets measured and does not *"slip through the cracks."*

2   26. We gather data automatically (*e.g., does not require extra manual labor*) whenever appropriate.

2   27. Data is gathered close in time to the performance event (*e.g., recorded immediately rather than two weeks later*).

2   28. We link process measures to customer requirements.

3   29. The method to communicate measurement data to employees is very effective.

2   30. We review measurement data at management meetings and we take quality improvement actions.

4   31. Data is presented graphically to help identify important trends.

4   32. We track quality performance for internal operations.

4   33. We track quality performance for products produced and services.

2   34. We track quality performance for *"key"* suppliers.

2   35. We measure customer satisfaction for each *"core"* market segment.

1   36. We measure employee morale and job satisfaction systematically.

1   37. Customer satisfaction measurements capture key information that accurately reflects customer preferences.

2   38. We continually evaluate and improve our measures and the methods used to collect and report performance data.

2   39. We have a way to summarize all our Key Result Areas easily.

2   40. We pay as much attention to the *"non-financial"* measures as we do to the financial measures.

Measurement System Self-Assessment Results

Out of a total of 200 possible points...

the executive team's average score was 92. They humbly agreed that their measurement system needed an overhaul and commented that the self-assessment was *"eye-opening."* They also agreed to pilot test the revised system in the Order Fulfillment Department after they developed their organization-wide KRAs and KIs.

CHAPTER THREE WORKSHEET: ASSESSING YOUR CURRENT MEASUREMENT EFFORTS

Scoring And Interpreting Your Results

Photocopy and then have your team complete the Measurement System Self-Assessment in the Appendix. Then tally the scores and analyze the results as follows:

1. Total the scores for each respondent who provided you a completed self-assessment.

_____

_____

2. Add the scores for all respondents.

_____

_____

3. Divide the total by the number of respondents. This is your average self-assessment score.

_____

_____

4. Analyze and discuss the implications of the average score.

_____

_____

_____

_____

_____

_____

_____

_____

If your total score is between 180-200, there is little evidence that you need to improve your current measurement efforts. You may want to promote your measurement system and allow other organizations to learn from your approach.

If your score is between 150-179, you may be close to a systematic approach to measuring things in your organization. However, there is evidence that you should begin rethinking and realigning your measurement efforts.

If your score is 149 or less, rethinking and realigning your measurement efforts should be a high priority.

Note: You should interpret this self-assessment only as a rough indicator of the effectiveness of your current measurement efforts.

STEP 1: DEVELOP ORGANIZATION-WIDE KRAS, KIS, AND PERFORMANCE "TARGETS"

Set The Direction For Organizational Improvement Efforts

One of the greatest challenges facing leaders is to coordinate and align organization-wide improvement priorities. Without coordination and alignment of organizational improvement efforts, actual performance may result in *"individual good"* instead of the *"common good!"*

♦ **Individual good:** Doing whatever it takes to make you and your work group look good and succeed.

♦ **Common good:** Doing whatever it takes to make everybody at your organization look good and succeed.

Imagine what an orchestra would sound like if all the musicians played their best solos simultaneously. Although members would be doing their very best individually, the orchestra as a whole would be suboptimizing its maximum potential.

An organization composed of work groups and people focusing on the individual good is also *"suboptimizing"* its own full potential. An organization, like an orchestra, must coordinate its processes in pursuing its goals to achieve maximum performance.

Your organization can achieve the *"common good"* by ensuring that individual work group Key Result Areas and Key Indicators are linked and aligned with the organization's vision, mission, strategic plans, KRAs, KIs, and performance targets.

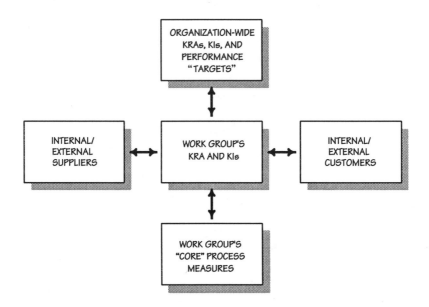

In the last chapter...

the executive team at Western Books, Inc. decided to pursue developing a *"reengineered"* system to measure organizational improvements. Their first step was to develop their organization-wide KRAs and KIs and then pilot test this process in the Order Fulfillment Department. The executive team developed the following KRAs and KIs based on their vision and mission.

Vision: Western Books, Inc. will be recognized worldwide by retailers and consumers as a world-class distributor of useful and practical information to help business leaders and employees achieve their maximum potential.

Mission: Western Books, Inc. distributes innovative and practical books to retailers and direct consumers worldwide. We will take any necessary steps to satisfy our customers' needs and exceed their expectations.

Based on their vision and mission statements, and after considerable discussion relating to strategic plans, the executive team agreed on the following KRAs and KIs....

KRA 1: Customer Loyalty
    KI 1: Number of *"compliment"* letters, calls, faxes, and e-mails/
        total number of books sold
    KI 2: Number of customer complaints resolved/total number of
        customer complaints
    KI 3: Percent rating in *"satisfied"* and *"very satisfied"* response
        categories on *"overall customer satisfaction"*

KRA 2: Quality
    KI 1: Defects/units of production
    KI 2: Order fulfillment cycle time
    KI 3: Number of correct shipments/total shipments

KRA 3: Innovation
    KI 1: Number of new product concepts in review
    KI 2: Number of suggestions submitted by employees/total number
        of employees
    KI 3: Number of suggestions implemented/total number of
        employees
    KI 4: Number of new products to market in the last 12 months/total
        products available

KRA 4: Productivity *(profit and revenue)*
    KI 1: Monthly gross profit margin
    KI 2: Average profit per product
    KI 3: Total revenue/total labor costs
    KI 4: Total revenue

KRA 5: Market Performance
    KI 1: Total number of customers
    KI 2: Total number of new customers per month
    KI 3: Number of products on top 10 best *"business books"*
    KI 4: Number of countries purchasing products

KRA 6: Quality of Work Life
    KI 1: Percent rating in top two of five response categories
        (Overall Employee Satisfaction Category)
    KI 2: Percent rating in top two of five response categories
        (Rewards And Recognition Satisfaction Category)
    KI 3: Percent of *"controllable"* turnovers *(turnover rate)*
    KI 4: Number of formal grievances/number of employees
    KI 5: Number of new hires recommended by employees/number
        of new hires

> KRA 7: Employee Growth and Development
> KI 1: Number of hours of training/total number of employees
> KI 2: Training costs/total budget
> KI 3: Number of promotions from within/total number of promotions
> KI 4: Performance appraisal rating scores

Develop Performance Targets

Organizations without clear performance targets are like a boat drifting on a *"horizonless"* ocean. Even with a strong wind, full sails, and a skilled crew, you won't know whether you succeeded if you didn't plot a specific course before setting out. Although you can argue that sailing is supposed to be fun, and can be done without a strict course and schedule to follow, the same cannot be said for the competitive business environment. Organizations need to know where they are going, and whether or not they've reached their destination. The more precisely *"where"* is defined, the greater the chance that the entire *"crew"* in the organization can fulfill their required roles.

Performance targets at the organizational level should:

♦ be *"descriptive"* without being overly *"prescriptive"* (they should provide clear direction but should not attempt to tell work groups how to accomplish the targets)

♦ focus on the organization's KRAs

♦ be *"high-level"* targets, reflecting a quantification of the organization's KIs

♦ be challenging, yet realistically achievable

Western's executive team...

also started to build their list of performance targets, some of which were already established in the organization's business plan. The group found it was relatively easy to set a year-end target for each KI after studying historical performance data, customer requirements research, and marketplace conditions.

KRA 1: Customer Loyalty

KI 1: Number of *"compliment"* letters, calls, faxes, and e-mails/total number of books sold

Performance Target: .03 level *(3 for every 100 books sold)*

KI 2: Number of customer complaints resolved/total number of customer complaints

Performance Target: 1.0 level *(100% of customer complaints will be resolved)*

KI 3: Percent rating in *"satisfied"* and *"very satisfied"* response categories on *"overall customer satisfaction"*

Performance Target: 95%

KRA 2: Quality

KI 1: Defects/units of production

Performance Target: Annual average of .05%; daily or batch average never to exceed 1%

KI 2: Order fulfillment cycle time

Performance Target: 98% of orders filled within 48 hours

KI 3: Number of correct shipments/total shipments

Performance Target: .998 level

Communicate The Direction

Once you've set your KRAs, KIs, and performance targets communicate them to everyone in the organization. Why everyone? Because everyone plays a role in getting things done. Customer satisfaction targets, for example, should not be confined to the sales, marketing, and product managers of an organization, since virtually everyone in an organization ultimately has an impact on overall customer satisfaction.

The same applies for other KRAs, KIs, and targets even if on the surface it appears that a particular target is only directly impacted by a certain work group. For example, the target of developing and securing patents on 12 new products a year may seem to fall within the domain of the Research and Development group only. But what about the role of others in the organization who support the R & D group? Those in purchasing, marketing research, and so on, as well as their internal suppliers, also contribute to the effort.

By widely communicating the direction throughout the organization, you:

◆ Clarify the organization's priorities and specific targets

◆ Help ensure that individual work groups are in alignment with the direction of the organization as a whole

◆ Convey the message that management has developed a well-thought-out plan

◆ Help work groups and individuals create their plans and establish priorities

CHAPTER FOUR WORKSHEET: CLARIFYING ORGANIZATION-WIDE KRAs, KIs, AND PERFORMANCE TARGETS

1. a. What is your organization's vision?

_____

_____

_____

_____

_____

_____

_____

b. What is its mission?

_____

_____

_____

_____

_____

_____

_____

2. What are the KRAs *(list from four to eight)* on which your organization needs to focus to achieve its vision and mission? *(Note: If these have not been formally established at the organization-wide level, list what you and your work group think they should be, then validate the list with management.)*

_____

_____

_____

_____

_____

_____

3. For each of these organization-wide KRAs, list the KIs that will serve as yardsticks for measuring progress.

_____

_____

_____

_____

_____

_____

_____

4. What are the organization's performance targets for each of these KIs. (*Note: Once again, if these targets have not been formally established, have your work group agree on what it thinks the targets should be and validate them with management.*)

_____

_____

_____

_____

_____

_____

5. How will you communicate this information? To whom should it be communicated?

_____

_____

_____

_____

_____

_____

STEP 2: SELECT ORGANIZATION-WIDE KRAS AND KIS LINKED TO YOUR WORK GROUP

The next step in the Measurement Linkage Model moves the focus from the organization-wide level to the work group level. Of course, not every work group will be translating each of the organization-wide KRAs and KIs into their own KRAs and KIs.

Departments, teams, and other work groups will need to select the KRAs and KIs to which they directly contribute. This selection process will require that you and your group:

♦ Understand your organization's vision and mission

♦ Identify how your work group functions as a system

♦ Link to organization-wide KRAs and KIs

The executive team at Western Books, Inc....

was ready to test their measurement system in the Order Fulfillment Department. Michelle Stames met with the manager of the Order Fulfillment Department, Lynda Gayle-Williams.

As the manager of the Order Fulfillment Department, Lynda Gayle-Williams oversees the processing of telephone and mail orders, and the answering of customer questions. Lynda decided she wanted to measure the effectiveness and efficiency of her work group since the current measurement system was not providing the information she and key people in her work group needed.

With Michelle's assistance, Lynda formed a *"Measurement Development Team"* (MDT) composed of six of her employees. Their charter: *"Develop a measurement system that helps their department monitor and track improvement efforts and to develop methods for collecting and feeding back information to the appropriate people."* …

To select the appropriate organization-wide KRAs and KIs, the members of a work group should:

---

1. Understand the key elements of their organization's vision and mission

2. Identify what their department produces in support of the vision and mission

3. Link their department's products and services and customer needs and expectations to the organization's KRAs

---

Understand Your Organization's Vision and Mission

Before you develop your measurement system, you must have a clear understanding of your organization's vision and mission and its KRAs and KIs. A facilitator should help you through this process. See how Michelle facilitates the Measurement Development Team's first meeting....

Michelle facilitated the MDT's first meeting...

while the group reviewed Western Books, Inc.'s vision and mission statements. They wrote the statements on a flip chart so they could identify the key phrases that related to their department's function.

Vision: Western Books, Inc. will be recognized worldwide by retailers and consumers as a world-class distributor of useful and practical information to help business leaders and employees achieve their maximum potential.

Mission: Western Books, Inc. distributes innovative and practical books to retailers and direct consumers worldwide. We will take any necessary steps to satisfy our customers' needs and exceed their expectations.

The MDT noted the key phrases in the vision and mission statements:
♦ A world-class distributor
♦ Help customers achieve maximum potential
♦ Distribute books
♦ Take any necessary steps to satisfy customer needs and expectations

Michelle pointed out to the MDT members that their department's measures must reflect these key elements outlined in the vision and mission statements....

Identify How Your Work Group Functions As A System

All work groups have customers, processes, and suppliers. Customers have needs and expectations. Work groups ("*producers*") have processes that produce products and services to satisfy those needs and expectations. Suppliers provide the necessary products and services to the work group.

A work group should gain a clear understanding of how it functions as a system of suppliers, producers, and customers. When the members of a work group understand how the group functions as a system, they will be better able to choose and develop appropriate measures that link to organizational improvement efforts.

Your Work Group As A "System"

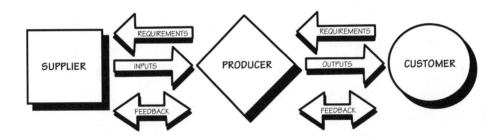

(Value-Added Processes)

The next step for the MDT...

was to understand how their department functioned as a system. Michelle drew a picture on a flip chart showing the relationship of suppliers, producers, and customers. Many of the MDT members had never thought of their department this way, but the model made sense to them. Michelle asked a series of questions to help the Order Fulfillment Department describe themselves as a system of suppliers, producer processes, and customers. The MDT brainstormed their answers to each question and Michelle recorded the information on flip chart paper....

When developing a picture of how your work group operates as a system, you should ask the following questions:

1. Whom does this work group serve? Who are our customers?

2. Rank these customers according to how important they are to our work group (*primary and secondary*).

3. What are our customers' needs and expectations?

4. What products/services does our work group produce to satisfy our customers' needs and expectations?

5. What processes do we have that provide those products and services?

6. What resources (*labor, energy, time, materials, etc.*) do we use as inputs to produce our products and services? Who provides these resources?

The MDT brainstormed...

their answers to these questions. Following group discussion and clarification, they agreed on the following *"picture"* of the Order Fulfillment Department as a system....

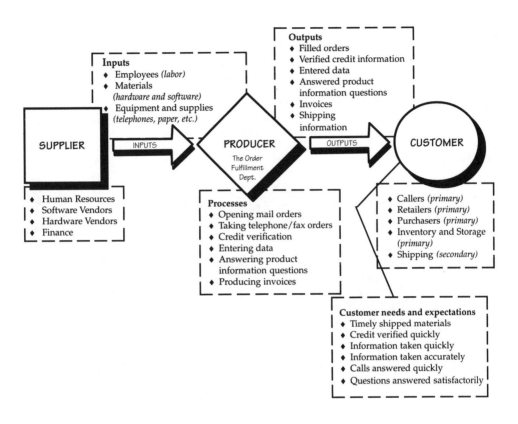

Link To Organizational KRAs and KIs

Once all members of a work group understand how they function as a system, they are ready to link themselves to the organization's KRAs and KIs. A work group can examine a list of the organization's KRAs and KIs and check off those that are related to its system of suppliers, inputs, processes, outputs, and customers.

Michelle listed Western Books' KRAs and KIs.

The MDT examined the list and checked off the KRAs and KIs that were linked to the work they did. The Order Fulfillment Department determined the following:

✔ KRA 1: Customer Loyalty
  ✔ KI 1: Number of *"compliment"* letters, calls, faxes, and e-mails/
       total number of books sold
  ✔ KI 2: Number of customer complaints resolved/total number of
       customer complaints
  ✔ KI 3: Percent rating in *"satisfied"* and *"very satisfied"* response
       categories on *"overall customer satisfaction"*

✔ KRA 2: Quality
    KI 1: Defects/units of production
  ✔ KI 2: Order fulfillment cycle time
  ✔ KI 3: Number of correct shipments/total shipments

  KRA 3: Innovation
    KI 1: Number of new product concepts in review
  ✔ KI 2: Number of suggestions submitted by employees/total
       number of employees
  ✔ KI 3: Number of suggestions implemented/total number of
       employees
    KI 4: Number of new products to market in the last 12 months/
       total products available

✔ KRA 4: Productivity *(profit and revenue)*
    KI 1: Monthly gross profit margin
    KI 2: Average profit per product
  ✔ KI 3: Total revenue/total labor costs
    KI 4: Total revenue

  KRA 5: Market Performance
    KI 1: Total number of customers
    KI 2: Total number of new customers per month
    KI 3: Number of products on top 10 best *"business books"*
    KI 4: Number of countries purchasing products

✔ KRA 6: Quality of Work Life
  ✔ KI 1: Percent rating in top two of five response categories
       (Overall Employee Satisfaction Category)

✔ KI 2: Percent rating in top two of five response categories
 (Rewards And Recognition Satisfaction Category)

✔ KI 3: Percent of *"controllable"* turnovers *(turnover rate)*

✔ KI 4: Number of formal grievances/number of employees

✔ KI 5: Number of new hires recommended by employees/
 number new hires

✔ KRA 7: Employee Growth and Development

  ✔ KI 1: Number of hours of training/total number of employees

  ✔ KI 2: Training costs/total budget

  ✔ KI 3: Number of promotions from within/total number of
  promotions

  ✔ KI 4: Performance appraisal rating scores

The MDT discovered that their work group's system was indeed linked to the organization-wide KRAs and KIs. However, not all of their products and services were linked. Michelle reassured the MDT that this was reasonable to expect since other departments in the organization produce products and services that had a direct link to some of the same and other KRAs and KIs.

When members of a work group determine how the group operates as a system, they can better link themselves to the organization's KRAs and KIs. Most work groups will directly link only a subset of the organization-wide KRAs and KIs. This is because top level KRAs and KIs must take the entire organization into consideration. When all work groups complete this process, an organization should check to see that all organization-wide KRAs and KIs are linked. Otherwise, there are gaps that will cause the achievement of important KRAs to *"slip through the cracks."*

When work groups complete this first step, they may encounter the need to create additional KRAs and KIs because of additional outputs and customers that are not encompassed as part of the organization-wide KRAs and KIs. We will see in the following chapters how to determine appropriate work-group specific KRAs and KIs.

CHAPTER FIVE WORKSHEET:
IDENTIFYING HOW YOUR WORK GROUP
FUNCTIONS AS A SYSTEM

To help you determine how your work group functions as a system, answer the following questions:

1. Whom is it that your work group was established to serve? Who are your customers?

_____

_____

_____

_____

_____

_____

2. Rank these customers according to how important they are to our work group *(primary and secondary)*.

_____

_____

_____

_____

_____

_____

3. What are our customers' needs and expectations?

_____

_____

_____

_____

_____

_____

_____

_____

4. What products/services does your work group produce to satisfy your customers' needs and expectations?

_____

_____

_____

_____

_____

_____

_____

_____

5. What processes do you have that provide those products and services?

_____

_____

_____

_____

_____

_____

6. What resources *(labor, energy, time, materials, etc.)* do you use as inputs to produce your products and services? Who provides these resources?

_____

_____

_____

_____

_____

_____

_____

7. Draw your work group as a system using the system diagram found in the Appendix.

8. Review your *"work group as a system"* diagram. If your organization has organization-wide KRAs and KIs, list them below. *(If not, skip to the next chapter.)* Check off the KRAs and KIs that you believe are linked to your work group. Pay particular attention to the link between your work group's outputs and customers' needs and expectations.

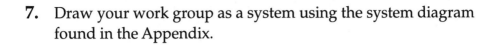

_____

_____

_____

_____

_____

_____

_____

_____

_____

_____

_____

_____

STEP 3: DEVELOP WORK GROUP "KEY RESULT AREAS"

Work group KRAs are critical, *"must-achieve," "make-or-break"* performance outcomes for which your work group is accountable. They categorize the major outputs produced by a work group to make its contribution to the organization. As you learned previously, some work group KRAs are directly linked *(and "titled")* the same as some of the organization-wide KRAs. If your work group produces any major outputs *(which are "value-added")* that do not directly support one of the organization-wide KRAs, you will need to develop one or more KRA categories which address these outputs.

Some examples of KRAs are:

♦ Customer Satisfaction

♦ Financial Performance

♦ Employee Satisfaction

♦ Operational Efficiency

♦ Public Responsibility

The characteristics of work group KRAs are:

♦ Business result areas that contribute to achieve an organization's strategic goals.

♦ They are aligned with the organization's strategic business plans.

♦ They are defined in terms of outputs, not inputs.

♦ They are defined as results, not processes, activities, or resources.

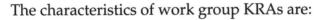

When developing work group-specific KRAs, you need to answer the following question:

 "On what do we focus to ensure our success?"

The outputs and customer needs and expectations, all determined while mapping out your work group as a system, should ultimately fall into a KRA category. If members of a work group have a set of organization-wide KRAs from which to work, their task is to link the KRAs to their work group's system. This situation is the typical one in most cases.

However, two special situations should also be considered. The first is when a work group needs to categorize additional KRAs if the organization's KRAs do not adequately address its products, services, and customer needs and expectations. The second is when a work group needs to develop its own KRAs because there are none at the organization-wide level.

Developing Work Group KRAs
Two Special Situations

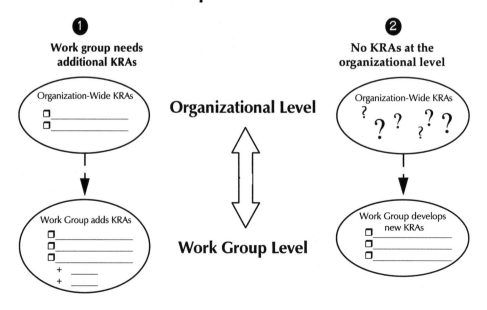

Develop Work Group KRAs

In both cases, a work group will follow these steps:

> KRA Step 1: Ask the fundamental KRA question
>
> KRA Step 2: Silently generate answers
>
> KRA Step 3: List answers in round-robin fashion
>
> KRA Step 4: Discuss and clarify list of possible KRAs
>
> KRA Step 5: Rank KRAs and reach a consensus

This is the same process an executive level team could use to develop organization-wide KRAs.

The following case study describes a work group developing KRAs on their own, without the benefit of having organization-wide KRAs to draw upon.

At a large software development company...

Staff Education and Training has developed KRAs for their department. Andy Tanner, the department director, formed a team to develop the work group's KRAs. Pamela Best, their "*star*" facilitator, facilitated the team in developing their KRAs. The team went through the first two steps in the 8-step measurement development process which included identifying how their work group functions as a system. Since they did not have organization-wide KRAs to link their "*system*" to, they developed their own KRAs from scratch. They used the Nominal Group Technique to agree upon their KRAs....

KRA Step 1: Ask the fundamental KRA question

A facilitator should use the Nominal Group Technique (*see explanation in Appendix*) to initiate this process with the team. The facilitator should write the following question on a flip chart or in a form that everyone can clearly see: "*On what do we focus to ensure our success?*"

Pamela wrote the question on...

flip chart paper and hung it on the conference room wall. The team took time to review the question. Most of the team members never thought of looking at their work group from this perspective....

KRA Step 2: Silently generate answers

Next, the facilitator should ask that the team members generate their own answers to the question posed in Step 1. The silent generation of answers stimulates thinking among the members. This is an important step, since it serves as the foundation for the development of the entire measurement system. The facilitator should allow the team ten to fifteen minutes to generate their answers.

The work group silently generated...
their answers to the question posed by Pamela. She allowed enough time for team members to write down their answers. The process of observing others write down answers stimulated creative thinking among team members....

KRA Step 3: List answers in round-robin fashion

In this step, the facilitator needs to record the work group's answers as quickly as possible on a flip chart. During this round, there is no criticism or discussion of the answers generated by the work group members. The facilitator lists the answers while the members read off one of their KRAs in a round-robin fashion. This continues until the facilitator records all possible KRAs.

Some team members were tempted...
to remark on the KRAs. Beckie thinks Dana's ideas are excellent and wants to praise her creativity. Pamela, however, recognizes that this praise will influence how others may think about Dana's KRAs and this may bias their rankings later. Pamela reminds the team members that they need to hold their comments back at this point in the process.

The team listed the following potential KRAs:

1. Provide quality training to customers
2. Provide training in quality facilities
3. Maintain good information
4. Maintain a positive culture and climate
5. Provide innovative ways of educating staff
6. Provide training and education productively
7. Meet and exceed customer requirements
8. Generate a maximum amount of revenue
9. Be able to tell our boss like it is
10. Make productive/efficient use of available resources
11. Measure productivity for our organization
12. Maintain documentation of policies and procedures
13. Act as role models for the organization
14. Develop our internal staff so they grow and prosper
15. Consultation to technical staff
16. Provide good food at seminars
17. Maintain excellent training equipment
18. Maintain enough people to provide excellent service
19. Fiscal accountability
20. Maintain good documentation
21. Positive cash flow
22. Respond in a timely manner
23. Attract the best people
24. Provide new programs
25. Live our values
26. Efficient use of resources
27. Provide excellent programs
28. Facilitate the company as being a fun place to work

KRA Step 4: Discuss and clarify list of possible KRAs

Once the facilitator lists all the KRAs, the work group should discuss and review the list. The purpose is to modify the KRAs to eliminate redundancy and improve their clarity and specificity. Typically, this process may eliminate twenty to thirty percent of the KRAs.

Revised List	Comments/Revisions
1. Provide quality training to customers	# 27 redundant with #1. Use # 1.
2. Provide training in quality facilities	
3. Maintain good information	# 12, 20 redundant with #2. Use #3
4. Maintain a positive culture and climate	
5. Provide innovative ways of educating staff Rewrite to: Provide new programs and innovative ways of educating staff	#24 similar to # 5. Rewrite # 5.
6. Provide training and education productively	# 19 redundant with #6. Use # 6.
7. Meet and exceed customer requirements	
8. Generate a maximum amount of revenue	
9. ~~Be able to tell our boss like it is~~ Rewrite to: Maintain positive climate to foster two-way communication	
10. Make productive/efficient use of available resources	# 26 redundant with # 10. Use # 10.
11. Measure productivity for our organization	
12. ~~Maintain documentation of policies and procedures~~	
13. Act as role models for the organization	
14. Develop our internal staff so they grow and prosper	
15. Consultation to technical staff	
16. Provide good food at seminars	
17. Maintain excellent training equipment	

Revised List	Comments / Revisions
18. Maintain enough people to provide excellent service	
~~19. Fiscal accountability~~	
~~20. Maintain good documentation~~	
21. Positive cash flow	
22. Respond in a timely manner	
23. Attract the best people	
~~24. Provide new programs~~	
25. Live our values	
~~26. Efficient use of resources~~	
~~27. Provide excellent programs~~	
28. Facilitate the company as being a fun place to work	

In this step, the team may combine some items with others, or rewrite some to make them more clear. It is important that the group understands they are still not to criticize or comment on how much they like the KRAs. They are only to learn the meaning behind them and clarify the list.

Pamela, the facilitator...

asked the team to combine any KRAs that are redundant. She also reviewed each potential KRA and asked the team members if they all understood the meaning behind them. Based on this discussion and clarification round, they came up with a revised list.

The team rewrote # 5 and # 9 and eliminated several redundancies. They can now rank the remaining KRAs to narrow the list even further.

KRA Step 5: Rank KRAs and reach a consensus

The team must now select from this list the KRAs that they feel are the most important for their work group. A work group should typically select four to seven KRAs. This number helps the group maintain focus and specificity.

First, the team members should pick their top five choices and rank each of these. The facilitator may use 3 X 5 cards to allow the group members to rank their KRAs. Next, the team members should write the number of the potential KRA in the top left-hand corner and the rank of the KRA in the bottom right corner. Five is the top ranking and one is the lowest.

Pamela asked the team members...

to choose their top five KRAs. *"Write the number of the KRA in the top left-hand corner,"* she began, *"and list the rank in the bottom right-hand corner. Five is your first choice; one is your fifth choice."* She handed out the cards, and the team got to work. The following list reveals their choices.

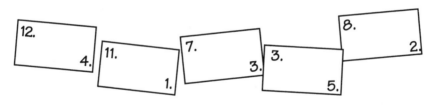

Revised List	Voting Pattern	Number Voting: Total Score
1. Provide quality training to customers	3-4-4-2-5-5	6:23
2. Provide training in quality facilities	1-1	2:2
3. Maintain good information	2	1:2
4. Maintain a positive culture and climate	3-2-1	3:6
5. Provide new programs and innovative ways of educating staff	2-3-4-4	4:13
6. Provide training and education productively	5-2-3-5-5-3-3	7:26

Revised List	Voting Pattern	Number Voting: Total Score
7. Meet and exceed customer requirements	5-4-4-3-2-1-4	7:23
8. Generate a maximum amount of revenue	none	none
9. Maintain positive climate to foster two-way communication	none	none
10. Make productive/efficient use of available resources	none	none
11. Measure productivity for our organization	2	1:2
12. Maintain documentation of policies and procedures	none	none
13. Act as role models for the organization	none	none
14. Develop our internal staff so they grow and prosper	1-1	2:2
15. Consultation to technical staff	none	none
16. Provide good food at seminars	1	1:1
17. Maintain excellent training equipment	none	none
18. Maintain enough people to provide excellent service	none	none
19. Fiscal accountability	none	none
20. Maintain good documentation	none	none
21. Positive cash flow	none	none
22. Respond in a timely manner	none	none
23. Attract the best people	none	none
24. Provide new programs	none	none
25. Live our values	none	none
26. Efficient use of resources	none	none
27. Provide excellent programs	none	none
28. Facilitate the company as being a fun place to work	none	none

The team noticed that four items...

on the list stood out as the top ones. They included:

	TOTAL SCORE
1. Provide quality training to customers	23
5. Provide new programs and innovative ways of educating staff	13
6. Provide training and education productively	26
7. Meet and exceed customer requirements	23

They agreed that these four should be the critical result areas for their work group. After reducing the larger list down to the these four, the group was now able to reword the items into more specific KRA category headings. They were respectively reworded as:

KRA 1: Quality Training   KRA 3: Productivity

KRA 2: Innovative Learning   KRA 4: Customer Satisfaction

Sometimes, conducting a second vote may be necessary, such as when a group cannot reduce the number of KRAs below seven or eight. In this case, the group should vote only on those KRAs that receive a relatively high ranking. For example, a group may have narrowed the list from fifty to twelve items in the first vote. The group members would then vote on the remaining 12 items.

Identify Your Work Group's KRAs

If you need to develop KRAs for your work group and you do not have organization-wide KRAs to serve as a guideline, you should have an experienced facilitator or consultant lead you through the five steps below:

1. Facilitator poses the fundamental question to the work group: *"On what do we focus to ensure our success?"*

2. The work group silently generates their answers.

3. The work group lists their answers in a round-robin fashion.

4. The work group discusses and clarifies their list of possible KRAs.

5. The work group ranks the KRAs through a special voting procedure to reach a consensus.

CHAPTER SIX WORKSHEET:
ADDING KEY RESULT AREAS

This worksheet is appropriate for work groups to list the organization-wide KRAs they have linked into during Step 2 of the Measurement Linkage Model. If no organization-wide KRAs exist or a work group determines that the organization-wide KRAs do not fully describe how they function as a system, the group members will need to develop work group-specific KRAs to help measure what they do. List the *"full plate"* of KRAs for your work group below.

KRA 1

KRA 2

KRA 3

KRA 4

KRA 5

KRA 6

KRA 7

STEP 4: DEVELOP WORK GROUP "KEY INDICATORS"

Once a work group determines its KRAs, the next step is to develop the KIs for each KRA. A KI is a concrete measure of how well a work group is doing in a given KRA category. Each KRA typically has several KIs which, when analyzed both individually and collectively, provide an accurate, complete picture of how well you are progressing in that result area.

What Are Key Indicators (KIs)?

KIs are measures that determine how well a work group is accomplishing a KRA (*established at organization-wide and work group level*).

When developing KIs, your work group should answer the following questions:

> **℘** What concrete measure could be used to show how your work group is doing on each KRA?
>
> **℘** What would you point to if your boss asked you how you are doing in each KRA?

Characteristics of effective KIs include:

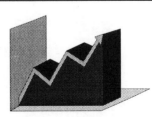

- ◆ Provides critical/important data
- ◆ Easily understood
- ◆ Controllable by your actions
- ◆ Tracks actual performance change
- ◆ Aligns with existing data or can be "*clearly*" established
- ◆ Measures efficiency (*timeliness, throughput, quantity, etc.*) and/or effectiveness (*impact, quality, contribution, etc.*)

Some examples of KIs include:

- Number of customer complaints successfully resolved ÷ number of customer complaints received x 100 (*efficiency-oriented*)

- Customer retention rate (*number of previous customers ÷ number of total customers*) per year (*effectiveness-oriented*)

- Sales per employee (*efficiency-oriented*)

- Net profit per employee (*effectiveness-oriented*)

- Employee Satisfaction Index (*based on items #3, 8, 28, 42, and 50 from Employee Opinion Survey*) level (*effectiveness-oriented*)

- Number of employee survey responses this year ÷ number of employee survey responses last year (*efficiency-oriented*)

Develop Work Group KIs

There are several important steps in developing good KIs to measure your work group's performance toward achieving its KRAs:

KI Step 1: Review work group KRAs

KI Step 2: Review "*linked*" KIs

KI Step 3: Ask the fundamental KI question for each KRA

KI Step 4: Silently generate answers

KI Step 5: List answers in round-robin fashion

KI Step 6: Discuss and clarify list of possible KIs

KI Step 7: Rank KIs and reach a consensus

The process of developing KIs is similar to that of developing KRAs *(as described in Chapter Six)*. A facilitator is used to keep the work group on target and the Nominal Group Technique helps identify the KIs. The main difference is that the group repeats the process for each KRA. Thus, it will take more time to develop KIs than it does to develop KRAs. You should try to tackle no more than one or two sets of KIs at a time.

KI Step 1: Review work group KRAs

The work group should understand the KRAs before developing their KIs. Each KRA represents a different *"chunk"* of the products, services, and outcomes of a work group's system. Everyone on the team should clearly understand the KRAs.

When getting started with each round of KI development for each KRA, the facilitator should write the following question on flip chart paper or in a form that everyone can clearly see: *"What do we measure to determine how successful we are in achieving this Key Result Area?"*

Michelle, the MDT's facilitator...

at Western Books, Inc. listed the Order Fulfillment Department's KRAs on flip chart paper. She wrote:

- ◆ Customer Loyalty
- ◆ Quality
- ◆ Innovation
- ◆ Productivity *(profit and revenue)*
- ◆ Quality of Work Life
- ◆ Employee Growth and Development

Michelle asked if there were any questions about their meaning. Since her team was the same team that selected these KRAs earlier, there were very few questions. Michelle proceeded to the next step....

KI Step 2: Review *"linked"* KIs

When there are organization-wide KRAs to work from, there may be related KIs that a work group must report on. The work group should review those selected during Step 2 of the Measurement Linkage Model *(as described in Chapter 5)*.

Work groups that do not have organization-wide KRAs and KIs to work from should skip to KI Step 3.

Michelle listed the KIs...

the team previously chose as measures linked to their work group's system. They included:

✔ KRA 1: Customer Loyalty.
   ✔ KI 1: Number of *"compliment"* letters, calls, faxes, and e-mails/ total number of books sold
   ✔ KI 2: Number of customer complaints resolved/total number of customer complaints.
   ✔ KI 3: Percent rating in *"satisfied"* and *"very satisfied"* response categories on *"overall customer satisfaction"*

✔ KRA 2: Quality
   ✔ KI 2: Order fulfillment cycle time
   ✔ KI 3: Number of correct shipments/total shipments

✔ KRA 3: Innovation
   ✔ KI 2: Number of suggestions submitted by employees/total number of employees
   ✔ KI 3: Number of suggestions implemented/total number of employees

✔ KRA 4: Productivity (*profit and revenue*)
   ✔ KI 3: Total revenue/total labor costs

✔ KRA 6: Quality of Work Life
   ✔ KI 1: Percent rating in top two of five response categories (*Overall Employee Satisfaction Category*)
   ✔ KI 2: Percent rating in top two of five response categories (*Rewards And Recognition Satisfaction Category*)
   ✔ KI 3: Percent of *"controllable"* turnovers (*turnover rate*)
   ✔ KI 4: Number of formal grievances/number of employees
   ✔ KI 5: Number of new hires recommended by employees/number of new hires

✔ KRA 7: Employee Growth and Development
   ✔ KI 1: Number of hours of training/total number of employees

---

✔ KI 2: Training costs/total budget
✔ KI 3: Number of promotions from within/
total number of promotions
✔ KI 4: Performance appraisal rating scores

The team members found that sometimes they did not need to develop additional KIs *(e.g. KRA 1: Customer Loyalty, KRA 6: Quality of Work Life, and KRA 7: Employee Growth and Development)*. The linked organization-wide KIs were plenty and appropriate for their work group.

However, there were some KRAs that needed more KIs to adequately measure their work group's performance. For those KRAs, the team needed to generate additional KIs.

KI Step 3: Ask the fundamental KI question for each KRA

The process of developing work group level KRAs can fall out two ways. Either the work group has organization-wide KRAs and KIs to work from *(and possibly add to)*, or the work group must develop their own KRAs and KIs in absence of organization-wide ones. In both cases, a work group can use the following procedure either to generate additional KIs or to develop an entire new set of KIs.

The process begins by asking the fundamental KI question:

"What do we measure to determine how successful we are in achieving this KRA?"

The MDT needed to develop...

additional KIs for their quality, innovation, and productivity *(profit and revenue)* KRAs. The team decided to start with the productivity KRA. Michelle listed the KIs the team had earlier identified as those the team felt were linked to their work group.

✔ KRA 4: Productivity *(profit and revenue)*
✔ KI 3: Total revenue/total labor costs

Michelle posed the question to the team: *"What do we measure to determine how successful we are in achieving this KRA?"*...

KI Step 4: Silently generate answers

Once the facilitator poses the fundamental KI question, the work group silently generates potential KIs.

The MDT silently generated...

several potential KIs. Some team members finished in a few minutes. Others took up to fifteen minutes to complete their list. Michelle asked those who were finished to remain silent while others completed their lists.

KI Step 5: List answers in round-robin fashion

In this step, the facilitator records the work group's answers as quickly as possible on a flip chart. During this round, there is no criticism or discussion of the answers generated by the members of the work group. The facilitator lists the answers while the members read off one of their KIs in a round-robin fashion. All members take turns reading one of their KIs. This continues until the facilitator records all possible KIs. When a member runs out of KIs on his list, he says *"pass."*

The team generated the following KIs...

for the productivity *(profit and revenue)* KRA category:

---

1. Total revenue/total labor costs
    (This organization-wide KI was identified earlier as linked to the work group.)
2. Queue time *(in seconds)*
3. Percent of caller hang-ups while on hold
4. Expense control within budget
5. Reduction in operating costs
6. Total unit output revenue/total input costs
7. Number of PCs/employee
8. Call time/order amount
9. Net revenue/employee
10. Average meeting ratings
11. Number of meetings/month
12. Wait time/customer
13. Unit cost/customer

KI Step 6: Discuss and clarify list of possible KIs

The facilitator should lead the group to consider each indicator, one at a time. Indicators typically need to be refined. Less experienced work groups may confuse an indicator with a goal or objective. For example, they may list an indicator as *"zero defects."* This may be an ideal goal, but it is not the indicator. The correct indicator could be worded as *"the number of defects," "percentage of defects," "reject level,"* etc.

KI Step 7: Rank KIs and reach a consensus

This step of the process serves to eliminate undesirable and impractical KIs. The members of the work group use a criteria check-off list to determine which KIs they want to use.

Michelle asked the MDT to...
check each KI against the following criteria:

1. Will the organization be interested in this measure? *(Is it important?)*

2. Is the KI easily understood?

3. Will the KI help our work group manage its performance?

4. Is the data available or can it be collected?

5. Is the KI reliable?

6. Is the KI cost effective to collect?

The KIs and these criteria are placed in a criteria check-off list. Each potential KI is checked against the criteria questions listed on the previous page. The KIs that meet the criteria should be considered to measure performance on that KRA (*four or less KIs per KRA are recommended*).

The team looked at the list...

of KIs they brainstormed. They discovered that some KIs meet all the criteria while other KIs do not.

KRA: Productivity	CRITERIA QUESTION					
Potential KIs	1	2	3	4	5	6
*1. Total revenue/total labor costs	✔	✔	✔	✔	✔	✔
*2. Queue time	✔	✔	✔	✔	✔	✔
*3. Percent of caller hang-ups while on hold	✔	✔	✔	✔	✔	✔
4. Expense control within budget	✔	✔	✔	✔		✔
5. Reduction in operating costs	✔	✔				
6. Total unit output revenue / total input costs						
7. Number of PCs/employee		✔		✔	✔	✔
*8. Call time /order amount	✔	✔	✔	✔	✔	✔
9. Net revenue /employee	✔			✔	✔	✔
10. Average meeting ratings		✔	✔	✔		✔
11. Number of meetings/month		✔	✔	✔	✔	✔
12. Wait time/customer						
13. Unit cost/customer	✔			✔		✔

*KIs # 1, 2, 3, and 8 meet all the criteria. The team agreed that these were the appropriate KIs for their work group.

CHAPTER SEVEN WORKSHEET:
IDENTIFYING YOUR WORK GROUP'S KIs

Using the criteria check-off list below will help you select your KIs for each KRA you have developed. List the numbers corresponding to your selection criteria in the top row. In the first column, list the KIs your work group has generated. Then, for each KI, check the cells that meet the appropriate criteria. The KIs that have all the boxes checked should be considered.

KRA:	CRITERIA QUESTION					
Potential KIs	1	2	3	4	5	6

STEP 5: DETERMINE DATA COLLECTION, TRACKING, AND FEEDBACK METHODS

A Critical Consideration

Collecting and tracking the KI data is where *"the rubber meets the road"* and where many measurement attempts fail. Although you have laid the groundwork by identifying your work group's KRAs and KIs, it is critical that you track and monitor your data.

Determining how data will be collected requires a work group to answer the following questions:

> ？ Who will collect it?
>
> ？ How will it be collected?
>
> ？ Where will the data be stored and posted so that employees can monitor their performance?
>
> ？ When will it be collected and posted?

If the members of a work group are not clear on the answers to all these key questions, then they may fail in using their measurement data effectively.

Let us look at how the MDT...

at Western Books Inc. answered these questions. The Order Fulfillment Department manager, Lynda, assigned each member of the MDT to take on one KRA and answer the questions of *"who, how, where, and when"* for each KI.

The first one to complete the answers to these questions was Emily Gomez. Lynda appropriately assigned her the productivity *(profit and revenue)* KRA and had given each team member a blank KI Data Collection Worksheet to complete. As you recall, there were four key indicators for this KRA:

KI 1–Total revenue/total labor costs
KI 2–Queue time (*in seconds*)
KI 3–Percent of caller hang-ups while on hold
KI 4–Call time/order amount

Emily's worksheet listed the following:

KRAS/KIs	METHODS		TARGETS
KRA: Productivity *(profit and revenue)*			
KI 1: Total *(unit output)* revenue/total input costs *(labor)*	**Who:**	Accounting Department	TBD
	How:	Accounting tracks revenue as output and unit costs as input (*total direct and indirect labor costs*). Equipment not functioning is flagged in the database.	
	Where:	Accounting Department provides monthly report to Lynda Gayle-Williams, and she posts in break room.	
	When:	Quarterly	
KI 2: Queue time *(in seconds)*	**Who:**	Lynda Gayle-Williams	TBD
	How:	Telephone system tracks time automatically.	
	Where:	Lynda Gayle-Williams prints out results weekly, and she posts in break room.	
	When:	Weekly	
KI 3: Percent of caller hang-ups while on hold	**Who:**	Lynda Gayle-Williams	TBD
	How:	Telephone system tracks all incoming calls and those in which callers hang up while waiting on hold.	
	Where:	Lynda Gayle-Williams prints out data and posts in break room.	
	When:	Weekly	
KI 4: Call time *(seconds)*/ order amount	**Who:**	Unit Secretary *(Order Efficiency)*	TBD
	How:	Unit Secretary tabulates reports from the computer. Computer tracks the time of each call and the amount of the order associated with it.	
	Where:	Lynda Gayle-Williams summarizes data and posts in break room.	
	When:	Monthly	

Data Collection Tips

When developing your measurement system, you should consider holding employees accountable for data collection and reporting. This will help ensure that the data collection and reporting actually gets done. When this does not occur, data may *"slip through the cracks."*

You will also find that each KI may have its own natural *"time for tracking."* For example, some KIs are tracked *quarterly (e.g., employee turnover)* and others may be tracked *monthly (e.g., sales).* Use this natural timing to help determine when the data will be collected and posted.

You may find collecting and reporting data difficult at first. Be patient. It takes time to get your measurement system working the way you want it to.

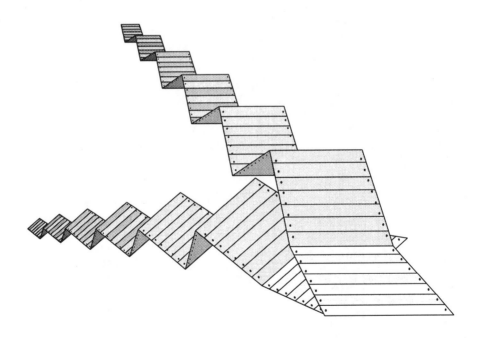

CHAPTER EIGHT WORKSHEET: DEFINING YOUR MEASUREMENT METHODS

1. Complete a KI Data Collection Worksheet for your work group's top KRAs. *(See Appendix for reproducible worksheet.)*

KRAs/KIs	METHODS	TARGETS
KRA:		
KI 1:	Who: How: Where: When:	
KI 2:	Who: How: Where: When:	
KI 3:	Who: How: Where: When:	
KI 4:	Who: How: Where: When:	

2. How will people be held accountable for collecting and
reporting the KI data?

_____

_____

_____

_____

_____

_____

_____

_____

_____

_____

_____

_____

_____

_____

_____

_____

_____

_____

STEP 6: GATHER "BASELINE" DATA AND SET PERFORMANCE "TARGETS"

Gather Baseline Data

Many organizations identify goals and objectives with inadequate knowledge of where they are now. Setting improvement goals without knowledge of how a process or system is performing is a prescription for disappointment.

A process can only produce a certain level of performance, in spite of the goal that is set for it. For example, a sprinter can only cover 100 meters in about ten seconds or so, despite his or her goal of cutting that time in half by next year! The *"process"* of sprinting is not capable of doing much better than that. The only way to improve that time is to change the process, not to set unrealistic goals. By the way, if the sprinter wants to cut his or her 100-meter dash time in half, driving might be the answer.

Many managers have unrealistic expectations of how much their work groups can improve, because they do not understand what their current processes or systems are capable of producing. With the best of intentions, they set targets that are not achievable while processes remain the same.

Gathering baseline data about the performance of work group processes and systems will help leaders set realistic performance targets.

Understand Where You Are Now

KIs are the measures that tell you *"where your processes or systems are"* at a given point in time. A performance target should be set based on knowledge of the capabilities of your processes or systems.

The Order Fulfillment Department's Productivity...

KRA had several KIs. One KI was the percent of caller hang-ups while waiting on hold. More specifically it was:

$$\frac{\text{Total \# of people who hang up during a work day}}{\text{Total \# of people who originally called in a work day}} \times 100\% = \begin{array}{l}\text{Daily \% of} \\ \text{hang-ups}\end{array}$$

Lynda wanted this number to be zero, but she knew it wasn't realistic, given the demands on her order entry operators. So she wasn't sure what the performance target should be. Fortunately, a computer tracked the telephone calls and the number of callers who had hung up. It was time for her to look at all those reams of paper the computer had spewed out over the past several months. She found that looking at this historical data to understand the actual performance of her telephone operators was easier than she expected.

The computer generated the reports at the end of each day and showed the number of caller hang-ups and the number of callers. She calculated the weekly average of caller hang-up rates for the past ten weeks. Ten weeks seemed like a reasonable amount of time to establish a baseline. Any heavy weeks would be balanced by slow weeks during that time. She discovered the following results:

	NUMBER OF CALLERS	NUMBER OF HANG-UPS	PERCENT OF HANG-UPS
Week 1	900	35	3.9%
Week 2	854	32	3.7%
Week 3	1453	125	8.6%
Week 4	708	10	1.4%
Week 5	899	42	4.7%
Week 6	997	57	5.7%
Week 7	889	60	6.7%
Week 8	921	49	5.3%
Week 9	900	26	2.9%
Week 10	936	45	4.8%
Average			4.8%

Lynda discovered that the average percent of callers who hang-up was 4.8. This was higher than she expected, but now she knew how many callers typically hang up each week.

The numbers by themselves did not look like much in the raw form so Lynda put the data in a run chart to make more sense out of it. She saw the following:

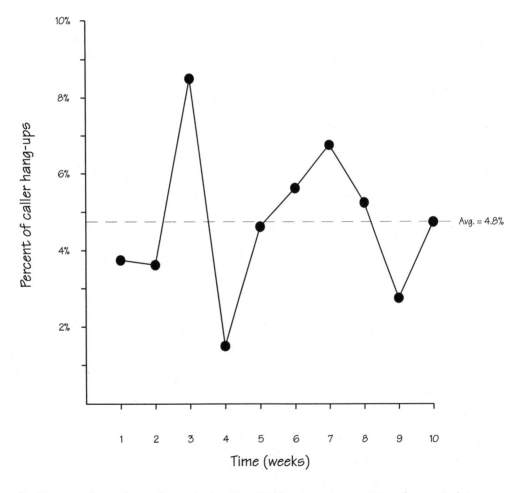

The run chart showed a variation in caller hang-up percentages from week to week, but the hang-ups averaged about 4.8 percent. There were no obvious patterns in the data so Lynda felt there was nothing unusual about the sample.

Set Realistic Performance Targets

You can set realistic performance targets once you have knowledge of how your processes and/or systems perform. Of course, setting a performance target does not ensure improvement. Reaching the performance target requires improving the process or system.

 Lynda's first impression...

of the data was that Week 4 was the Order Fulfillment Department's best week. She examined the run chart of the baseline data and saw that Week 4 had 1.4 percent hang-ups. She thought that 1.4 percent might be a reasonable target since her department had already achieved it. However, she also noticed that week was unusually slow and it followed a very busy week. She went back to her staffing records and noticed that there was an extra employee working that week. The combination of a slow week and extra operators made this week an unusual circumstance and not very representative of a typical week. The combination of fewer calls and extra staff may have resulted in fewer caller hang-ups.

The next best normal week was Week 9 at 2.9 percent. Lynda decided that 3 percent caller hang-ups was a reasonable target number for her department, for now. Of course, her department would continually work on its processes to reduce that number below 3 percent. Nevertheless, a 3 percent caller hang-up rate would be worth shooting for at first.

Do A "Reality Check" Of The Performance Targets

Having baseline data allows you to establish more realistic performance targets. However, it may prove worthwhile to bounce your targets off others to make sure they are realistic. You may share the targets with your manager or with the employees and get agreement that the targets are indeed realistic.

CHAPTER NINE WORKSHEET: ESTABLISHING PERFORMANCE TARGETS

Answer the following questions. They will help you to clarify information that you will need to establish realistic performance targets.

1. Among the KIs you have identified, which ones do you currently collect data on?

_____

_____

_____

_____

_____

2. For each KI, what is the baseline level of performance?

_____

_____

_____

_____

_____

_____

3. Among the KIs you have identified, which ones do you not
currently collect data on?

_____

_____

_____

_____

_____

_____

_____

_____

4. How will you gather data on each of these KIs?

_____

_____

_____

_____

_____

_____

_____

5. Considering your baseline data, what should be the performance target for each KI?

_____

_____

_____

_____

_____

_____

_____

_____

_____

_____

_____

_____

_____

_____

_____

STEP 7: ESTABLISH WORK GROUP "OBJECTIVES" AND "TACTICS"

Your work group is clear on its direction and knows which KIs to track as it moves forward. In this next step, your group needs to set specific objectives and the tactics the group will employ to reach those objectives.

Categories Of Work Group Objectives

Your group's tactics will vary according to the nature of the objectives, and can be grouped into the following partial list of common types or categories:

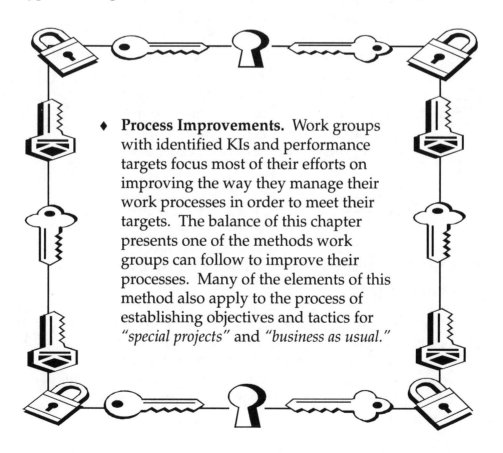

♦ **Process Improvements.** Work groups with identified KIs and performance targets focus most of their efforts on improving the way they manage their work processes in order to meet their targets. The balance of this chapter presents one of the methods work groups can follow to improve their processes. Many of the elements of this method also apply to the process of establishing objectives and tactics for *"special projects"* and *"business as usual."*

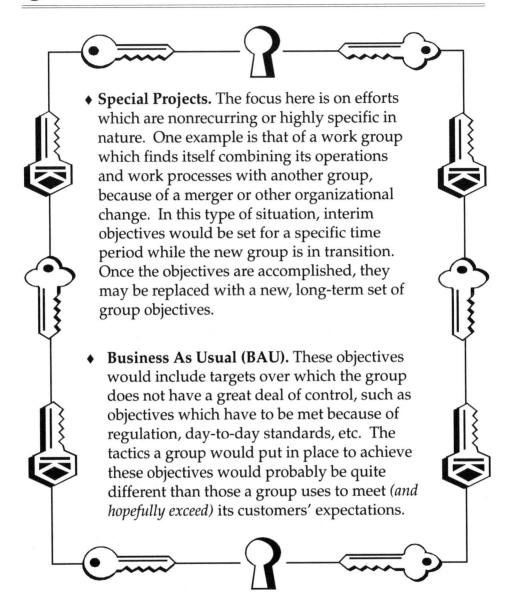

- **Special Projects.** The focus here is on efforts which are nonrecurring or highly specific in nature. One example is that of a work group which finds itself combining its operations and work processes with another group, because of a merger or other organizational change. In this type of situation, interim objectives would be set for a specific time period while the new group is in transition. Once the objectives are accomplished, they may be replaced with a new, long-term set of group objectives.

- **Business As Usual (BAU).** These objectives would include targets over which the group does not have a great deal of control, such as objectives which have to be met because of regulation, day-to-day standards, etc. The tactics a group would put in place to achieve these objectives would probably be quite different than those a group uses to meet *(and hopefully exceed)* its customers' expectations.

Establish Objectives And Tactics For Process Improvements

Once you identify your KIs and performance targets, beginning your process improvement effort is easy. The model recommended is the "SAMIE™" model, which is a continuous process improvement method. Many steps you complete in developing your measurement system lay the groundwork for process improvement.

THE SAMIE™ MODEL

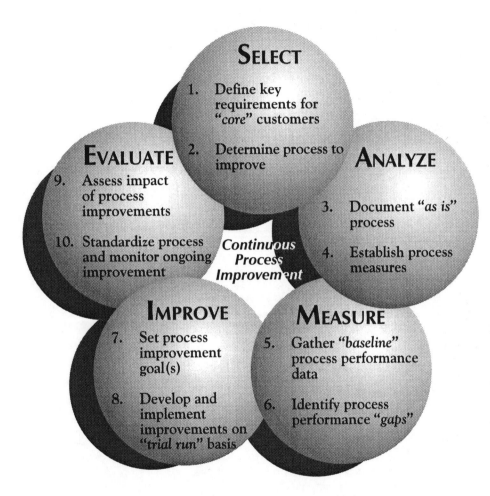

As you can see, the SAMIE model follows ten basic steps. Let's bring the Order Fulfillment Department back into the picture and see how the department employees apply the SAMIE model to their measurement efforts.

Note: *Continuous Process Improvement* and *Continuous Improvement Tools Volumes I and II* are other practical guidebooks by Richard Chang Associates, Inc. that offer additional information on the SAMIE model.

Select

1. Define key requirements for *"core"* customers

The work group already completed this in Step 1. They identified their core customers as:

♦ Callers (*Primary*)
♦ Retailers (*Primary*)
♦ Purchasers (*Primary*)
♦ Inventory and Storage (*Primary*)
♦ Shipping (*Secondary*)

Their requirements were identified as:
♦ Timely shipped materials
♦ Credit verified quickly
♦ Information taken quickly
♦ Information taken accurately
♦ Calls answered quickly
♦ Questions answered satisfactorily
♦ Telephone representatives are friendly and courteous
♦ Shipping information is timely
♦ Shipping information is accurate
♦ Callers do not have to wait too long on hold

2. Determine process to improve

The Order Fulfillment Department wanted to improve its telephone answering process *(from point of call receipt to point of customer question being answered or placement of an order)*. Lynda Gayle-Williams assigned several members from her department to study and improve the process. She was able to choose this process easily since it was a KI for the Productivity *(profit and revenue)* KRA.

Analyze

3. Document *"as is"* process

The team developed an *"as is"* flow chart:

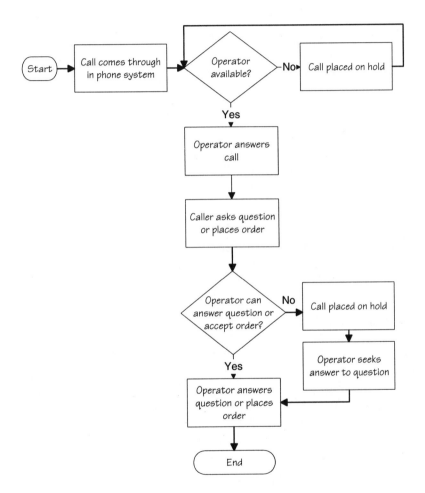

4. Establish process measures

The process measure is the KI which was already established. It is:

$$\frac{\text{Total \# of people who hang up during a work day}}{\text{Total \# of people who originally called in a work day}} \times 100\% = \begin{array}{l}\text{Daily \% of}\\\text{hang-ups}\end{array}$$

Measure

5. Gather *"baseline"* process performance data
The MDT completed this in Step 5. The baseline data shows an average of 4.8 percent.

6. Identify process performance *"gaps"*
The *"gap"* is the difference between the percent of caller hang-ups *(at 4.8 percent)* and the target of less than 3.0 percent.

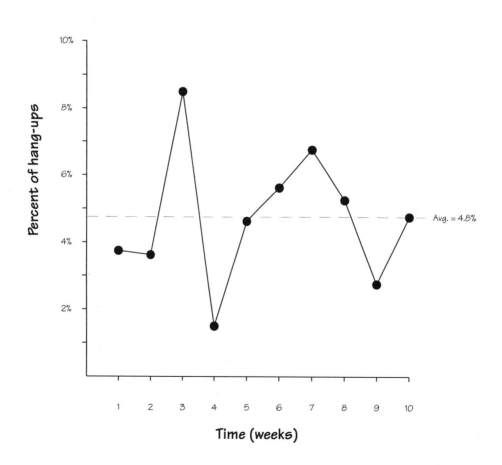

Improve

7. Set process improvement goal(s)

The team's goal was to improve the process so there are less than 3.0 percent caller hang-ups by the end of next quarter.

8. Develop and implement improvements on *"trial run"* basis

The team identified through the flow chart that there were two times when a caller was placed on hold. Therefore, a caller had the *"opportunity"* to hang up twice. The hang-up was directly related to the amount of time a caller must wait on hold. The solution seemed simple. Shorten the time callers must wait on hold, and put them on hold as few times as possible.

The team brainstormed some reasons why an operator may not get back to a caller in a timely manner. They used a Cause and Effect diagram and discovered the following:

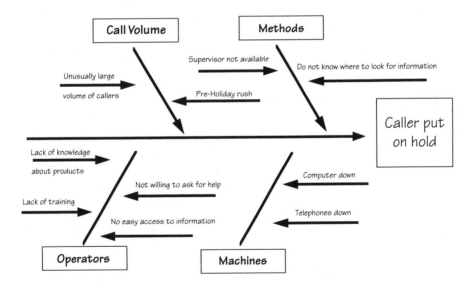

The team felt the greatest cause of delays was when an operator put the caller on hold because she did not know the answer to a question. The team recommended that the Order Fulfillment Department operators have access to a list of answers to frequently-asked questions.

Lynda thought this was a terrific idea, and she had the operators keep track of frequently-asked questions so they could generate the list. They generated the list, developed a job-aid card with answers to the top 15 questions, and held a brief training session to cover them with the operators.

Evaluate

9. Assess impact of process improvement

The number of caller hang-ups went down significantly. Only four weeks after implementing the list of frequently-asked questions and their answers, the average caller hang-up rate went from 4.8 percent to 2.4 percent.

10. Standardize process and monitor ongoing improvement

This process improvement effort was a success. The number of caller hang-ups went from 4.8% to 2.4%—a 50% improvement! The frequently-asked question sheet was expanded and is continually being updated.

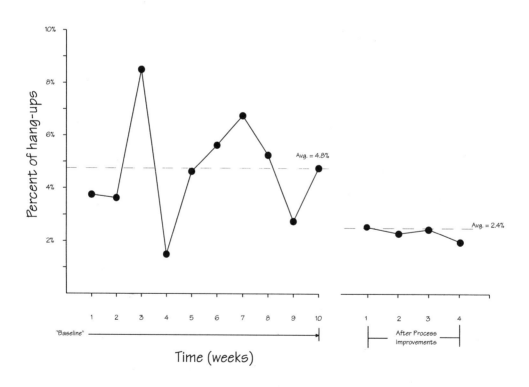

"Baseline" Data...	Number of Callers	Number of Hang-ups	Percent of Hang-ups
Week 1	900	35	3.9%
Week 2	854	32	3.7%
Week 3	1453	125	8.6%
Week 4	708	10	1.4%
Week 5	899	42	4.7%
Week 6	997	57	5.7%
Week 7	889	60	6.7%
Week 8	921	49	5.3%
Week 9	900	26	2.9%
Week 10	936	45	4.8%
After Process Improvement Implementation...			
Week 1	932	24	2.6%
Week 2	843	19	2.3%
Week 3	989	25	2.5%
Week 4	893	20	2.2%

As you can see, completing the measurement development steps has several positive side effects.

- ♦ Customers and their needs and expectations are identified.

- ♦ It is easier to select process improvement projects because the work group knows what is important.

- ♦ Data is already available for process improvement monitoring.

Linking your work group's processes to KRAs and KIs makes it easier to identify and improve internal work processes since the measures are linked to organization-wide KRAs.

CHAPTER TEN WORKSHEET:
IMPLEMENTING YOUR IMPROVEMENTS

1. Which of the 10 steps of the SAMIE model have you already completed?

_____ 1. Define key requirements for *"core"* customers.

_____ 2. Determine process to improve.

_____ 3. Document *"as is"* process.

_____ 4. Establish process measures.

_____ 5. Gather *"baseline"* process performance data.

_____ 6. Identify process performance *"gaps."*

_____ 7. Set process improvement *"goals."*

_____ 8. Develop and implement improvements on *"trial run"* basis.

_____ 9. Assess impact of process improvements.

_____ 10. Standardize process and monitor ongoing improvement.

2. Which steps do you still need to focus on? Develop your action plan to complete those steps, identifying what needs to be done, the time frame, who will do it, and the estimated cost.

_____

_____

_____

_____

_____

_____

_____

_____

_____

_____

_____

_____

_____

_____

_____

_____

_____

_____

STEP 8: IMPLEMENT PLANS, MONITOR PERFORMANCE, AND PROVIDE FEEDBACK

Provide Feedback To Appropriate Managers/ Employees Continually

In this last step, you will monitor performance of your work group continually. If you complete the process of establishing where and how you will post and report the data, you will have no problem doing this. Employees will appreciate the continual feedback and will use this information to improve their performance.

Managers need information on the performance of their work group so they can track performance. You may find that your reports will get much shorter because your managers will be asking you for performance data on your KIs, and not for the other, less important information. This is often a pleasant side benefit to using this type of measurement system.

Review And Revise Measurement System

Like all processes, your measurement system needs to be monitored to make sure it is providing reliable and valid information. In addition, as the goals of the organization and your work group change, so too must your measures. You may want to evaluate your measurement system annually, about one to two months before your annual planning/budgeting process.

Develop A KRA Tracking Matrix To Report Results

You may have several KRAs (*and several KIs within each*) to track at the work group level. The total number of KIs may provide too much information to give managers and employees a quick snapshot of how the organization and/or work group is doing. A KRA Tracking Matrix can be developed to provide a means of tracking and reporting changes in:

♦ individual KI performance

♦ total KRA performance based on a summary of the KIs

In addition, the KRA Tracking Matrix allows you the option to "*weight*" each KI by its importance in helping to achieve the KRA.

NOTE: The calculation methodology for determining an "*Index Score*" is the same for a KRA or KI Tracking Matrix. In addition, a KRA or KI "*Index Score*" can be calculated at an organization-wide and/or work group level.

Devise a KRA Tracking Matrix

These first three steps will help you devise a KRA Tracking Matrix. (*See the completed example on page 104 and the blank form in the Appendix*)

Step 1

List the KRA and its related KIs in the top of each column.

Step 2

Identify the "*Common Performance Levels*" for each KI. This step is critical if you want to transform the individual KIs into a single index score for the KRA. The common performance levels are numbered from 0 (*the worst possible*) to 10 (*the target or desired performance level*). These levels are defined as follows:

♦ Define the baseline performance level for each KI. The baseline should be based on historical data, showing the typical operating level for that KI.

♦ Write the baseline level for each KI as a "*3*" on the scale of common performance levels.

♦ Establish performance levels for each KI for "0" on the common performance level scale. Level 0 should be set at the lowest conceivable level of performance that reasonably might occur on the KI in question.

♦ Repeat this step for a Level 10 on the common performance level scale. Level 10 should be set at a *"stretch"* beyond the target level established earlier. The target should be challenging, yet achievable.

♦ Fill in the remaining values. Now that Levels 0, 3, and 10 have been determined for each indicator, the remaining common performance levels can be added. One way is to establish equal intervals between the baseline and Level 10 and the baseline and Level 0. This assumes it is equally difficult to move up the scale from one unit to the next. If it is believed that moving up the scale gets progressively more difficult as you get closer to the top (*e.g., 7, 8, 9, 10*), the increments can be made larger at the lower levels and smaller near the top.

Step 3

Establish weights. It is likely that the KIs are not equally important in contributing to the accomplishment of the KRA. KIs may be weighted to reflect their varying individual contribution. This is done by dividing 100 points among the KIs.

Lynda asked her team to help...

create the KRA Tracking Matrix for the Productivity *(profit and revenue)* KRA, with its four KIs. Emily suggested starting with the third KI, daily percent of caller hang-ups, since they had just looked at caller hang-up data for a period of several weeks. *"Good idea,"* Lynda said. *"So our baseline level is the 4.8% average figure we came up with,"* she added, *"and we already set a target of 3%, so we just need to come up with the figures to assign to the other performance levels."* The group agreed that 10% would be the worst possible performance, so they set this as the "0" performance level. At the other end of the scale, they set 2.7 % as the "10," or *"stretch"* level.

> After some discussion on appropriate figures for the various performance levels for the other three KIs, the team agreed to do a bit more digging to come up with accurate baseline levels. *"Once we have the baseline figures, it will be easier to set the different performance levels,"* suggested Lynda. The group agreed to pull the numbers from various sources and reconvene for a brief meeting in a week to complete their matrix. *"But in the meantime, let's plug in the weights for the four different KIs,"* Emily said. *"I think the 'Total revenue/Total labor cost' ratio is the most important. How about 40 out of 100?"*...

Reporting Results

Once Steps 1 - 3 are complete, the KRA Tracking Matrix is ready for use. The following Steps 4 - 9 describe how you can use the KRA Matrix to report results.

Step 4

Obtain KI data for the current period. KI results for each indicator are written on the *"Current Period Performance"* line.

Step 5

Circle the number in the appropriate KI column that comes closest to the current performance figure. Read across the columns to obtain *"Common Performance Levels"* scores. This process is repeated for each of the KIs for the KRA being tracked.

Step 6

Obtain *"Values"* for each KI. These are obtained by multiply-ing the performance level score *(0 to 10)* by the assigned *"Weight"* for each KI. This is the weighted value for the KI.

Step 7

Add the weighted *"Values"* for each KI to obtain the *"Index"* score. This gives an overall score for the KRA which can range from 0 to 1,000. Note that a score of 300 represents an *"average"* rating. This is due to the fact that the baseline was set at a Common Performance Level of 3.

Step 8

Use the KRA Index score to assess improvement impact. You will need to compare your Index scores from one period to the next. For example, say the Index score for the current performance period is 525 and is 25 points higher than the last. There is a 5% improvement. This improvement is calculated by the formula below:

$$\text{Percent Improvement} = \left(\frac{\text{Current Performance} - \text{Previous Performance}}{\text{Previous Performance}} \right) \times 100\%$$

Example:

$$\text{Percent Improvement} = \left(\frac{525 - 500}{500} \right) \times 100\% = 5\%$$

Lynda and the rest of the team...

from the Order Fulfillment Department had pulled together the data they needed and completed their matrix before the beginning of the recently ended month. *"Now we can look at where we are on our productivity (profit and revenue) KRA compared to our baseline of 300,"* said Lynda as the group kicked off its meeting.

The group began with the figure they got from accounting for the first KI, which came in at 57%, and wrote it on the Current Performance line of the matrix. The team members then added the current figures for the other three KIs and looked down the chart to get the performance level score for each of their four KIs. *"This is a definite improvement, with scores of 6, 4, 4, and 6, compared with our baseline level of 3,"* Lynda pointed out. *"We must be doing things right so far."*

The team multiplied the performance level scores for each KI by their respective weights, and added the four weighted values to come up with a indexed score of 540 for the productivity KRA. *"Way to go, team!"* said Lynda, as the group began to discuss the results of their first KRA Tracking Matrix. *"Next month we'll be able to compare the index as well as the performance levels for each of the KRAs so we can start assessing our changes over time."*

KRA Tracking Matrix

Work Group: Order Fulfillment Department

Date: March 31, 199X

KRA: Productivity (profit and revenue)

	1	2	3	4
KI	Total revenue/ Total labor costs	Queue Time (in seconds)/	Daily caller hang-ups while on hold	Call time(seconds) /order amount (dollars)
CURRENT PERFORMANCE	57	11	4.4	6

COMMON PERFORMANCE LEVELS

54	0	2.7	1	←	10	("Stretch" Level)
54.5	1	3.0	2	←	9	("Target" Level)
55	2	3.3	3	←	8	
56	4	3.6	4	←	7	
(57)	6	3.9	(6)	←	6	
58	8	4.2	8	←	5	
59	(12)	(4.5)	10	←	4	
60	20	4.8	12	←	3	("Baseline" Level)
62	30	6.5	15	←	2	
65	45	8.2	20	←	1	
69	60	10.0	30	←	0	

PERFORMANCE LEVEL SCORE	6	4	4	6	
WEIGHT	40	15	15	30	**INDEX**
WEIGHTED VALUE	240	60	60	180	540

CHAPTER ELEVEN WORKSHEET: UPDATING YOUR MEASUREMENT SYSTEM

1. Reproduce and use the blank KRA Tracking Matrix form in the Appendix to monitor improvement for a selected KRA *(or more than one, depending on how many KRAs you are tracking)* for your work group.

2. How will the information in the completed matrix be communicated to your group and others who have a stake in the KRAs?

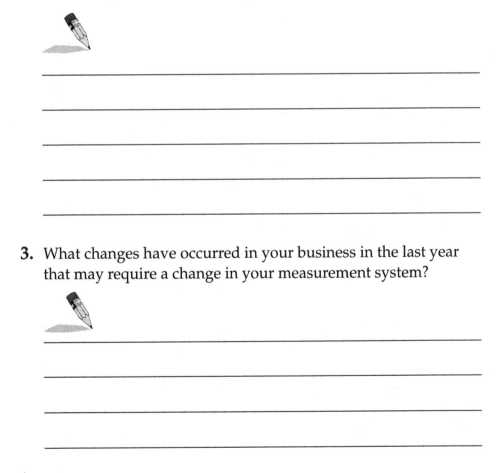

_____

_____

_____

_____

_____

3. What changes have occurred in your business in the last year that may require a change in your measurement system?

_____

_____

_____

_____

_____

CHAPTER TWELVE

SUMMARY

You have read about the model, and seen how the Measurement Development Team at Western Books, Inc. was able to successfully connect the day-to-day improvement efforts in the Order Fulfillment Department to the overall organizational vision and mission.

The measurement process begins with a clear picture of the organization's direction, defined in measurable terms as its KRAs, KIs, and performance targets *(Step 1)*.

Work groups within the organization then select those organization-wide KRAs and KIs on which the group can have an impact *(Step 2)*.

Each work group develops its own KRAs and KIs, reflecting the outputs they create and the processes they manage within the organization *(Steps 3 and 4)*.

Work groups then determine what data they will track, how they will collect it, and how measurement information will be communicated *(Step 5)*.

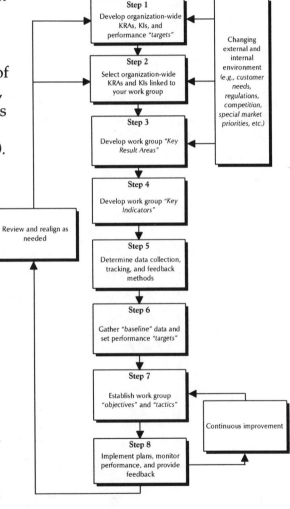

The next step has work groups establishing their starting points and their *"finish lines"* by collecting baseline data and setting performance targets *(Step 6)*.

Once the work groups and improvement teams have their starting points defined in measurable terms, they enter a cycle of continuous improvement. They set their specific improvement objectives and come up with the tactics they will use to accomplish these objectives *(Step 7)*, cycling back through the improvement process again and again, according to the improvements achieved towards their targets.

The final step *(Step 8)* has work groups and improvement teams implementing their plans and evaluating their results, thus feeding back into the continuous improvement process begun in the previous step.

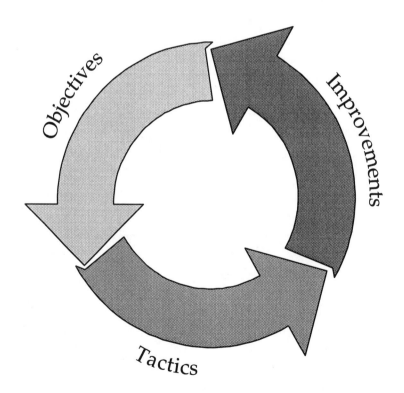

Organizational improvement has been described as the race without a finish. Although this analogy may inspire many of us, in the long run we all need to know how long the laps are, when the baton is handed off, and what the interim targets are. Otherwise, the challenge of a never-ending race can begin to wear us down.

By using the measurement model in this guidebook, you will be able to bring greater direction and definition, and thus greater success, to all your organizational improvement efforts.

REPRODUCIBLE FORMS AND WORKSHEETS

The pages in the Appendix are provided for you to photocopy and use appropriately.

Measurement System Self-Assessment

Rating Scale: Read each of the following statements. For each statement, rate our current measurement system based on the following response scale:

5 = Strongly Agree   4 = Agree   3 = Neither Agree Nor Disagree
2 = Disagree   1 = Strongly Disagree

_____ 1. Our current measurement system measures all the right things.

_____ 2. We collect measures linked to organizational improvement goals.

_____ 3. We define our measures from the customers' *"point of view."*

_____ 4. Our measurement system does not focus solely on *"bottom-line"* financial results.

_____ 5. This organization uses measurement data to promote continuous improvement and learning.

_____ 6. Our measurement system does not generate more paperwork than is necessary.

_____ 7. Our measurement system always gives us the information we need when we need it.

_____ 8. Our measurement system focuses on continuous improvement rather than compliance and control.

_____ 9. We are only accountable for measures for which we have control.

_____ 10. Our measures focus on the *"positive"* side rather than the *"negative"* side *(e.g., appointments met versus appointments missed).*

_____ 11. Our measurement system contains both objective and subjective measures.

_____ 12. Everyone understands the measures used to evaluate performance.

_____ 13. Managers or employees are accountable for measurement accuracy and results.

_____ 14. We act on measurement results quickly.

_____ 15. All data collection methods are cost-effective.

_____ 16. We always communicate measurement results to the appropriate managers and employees.

_____ 17. Our measures focus on effectiveness (*e.g., number of on-time arrivals*) and efficiency (*e.g., response time*).

_____ 18. All measures are reliable.

_____ 19. Senior leadership built our measurement system with a plan. It did not evolve by chance.

_____ 20. Measures show change when we make improvement efforts.

_____ 21. We have a method for screening out measures that we really do not use.

_____ 22. Our measurement system contains a *"well-balanced"* blend of KRAs reflecting our mission, vision, and strategic goals.

_____ 23. Our measurement system provides information that allows us to set clear objectives.

_____ 24. Objectives are based on a clear understanding of the performance capability of our systems and processes.

_____ 25. Important work that crosses functions gets measured and does not *"slip through the cracks."*

_____ 26. We gather data automatically (*e.g., does not require extra manual labor*) whenever appropriate.

_____ 27. Data is gathered close in time to the performance event (*e.g., recorded immediately rather than two weeks later*).

_____ 28. We link process measures to customer requirements.

_____ 29. The method to communicate measurement data to employees is very effective.

_____ 30. We review measurement data at management meetings and we take quality improvement actions.

_____ 31. Data is presented graphically to help identify important trends.

_____ 32. We track quality performance for internal operations.

_____33. We track quality performance for products and produced services.

_____34. We track quality performance for *"key"* suppliers.

_____35. We measure customer satisfaction for each *"core"* market segment.

_____36. We measure employee morale and job satisfaction systematically.

_____37. Customer satisfaction measurements capture key information that accurately reflects customer preferences.

_____38. We continually evaluate and improve our measures and the methods used to collect and report performance data.

_____39. We have a way to summarize all our Key Result Areas easily.

_____40. We pay as much attention to the *"non-financial"* measures as we do to the financial measures.

_____ Total Score   Name:_____ Date:_____

MEASUREMENT DEVELOPMENT SYSTEM CHECKLIST

Step 1: Develop Organization-Wide KRAs, KIs and Performance Targets

❑ Set the direction for Organizational Improvement Efforts

❑ Develop Performance Targets

❑ Communicate the direction

Step 2: Select Organization-Wide KRAs, KIs Linked To Your Work Group

❑ Understand your organization's vision and mission

❑ Identify how your work group functions as a system

❑ Link to organizational KRAs and KIs

Step 3: Develop Work Group Key Result Areas

❑ KRA Step 1. Ask the fundamental KRA question

❑ KRA Step 2. Silently generate answers

❑ KRA Step 3. List answers in round-robin fashion

❑ KRA Step 4. Discuss and clarify list of possible KRAs

❑ KRA Step 5. Rank KRAs and reach a consensus

Step 4: Develop Key Indicators

❑ KI Step 1. Review work group KRAs

❑ KI Step 2. Review *"linked"* KIs

❑ KI Step 3. For each KRA, ask:

"What do we measure to determine how successful we are in achieving this Key Result Area?"

❑ KI Step 4. Silently generates answers

❑ KI Step 5. List answers in round-robin fashion

❑ KI Step 6. Discuss and clarify list of possible KIs

❑ KI Step 7. Rank KIs and reach a consensus

Step 5: Determine Data Collection, Tracking, and Feedback Methods

❑ Who will collect the data?

❑ How will data be collected?

❑ Where will you store and post the data?

❑ When will the data be collected and posted?

Step 6: Gather Data And Set Performance Targets

❑ Gather baseline data

❑ Understand where you are now

❑ Set realistic performance targets

❑ Do a reality check of the performance targets

Step 7: Establish Work Group Objectives And Tactics

❑ Develop Action Plans to accomplish objectives

Step 8: Implement Plans, Monitor Performance, And Provide Feedback

❑ Provide feedback to appropriate managers/employees continually

❑ Review and revise measurement system

YOUR WORK GROUP SYSTEM DIAGRAM

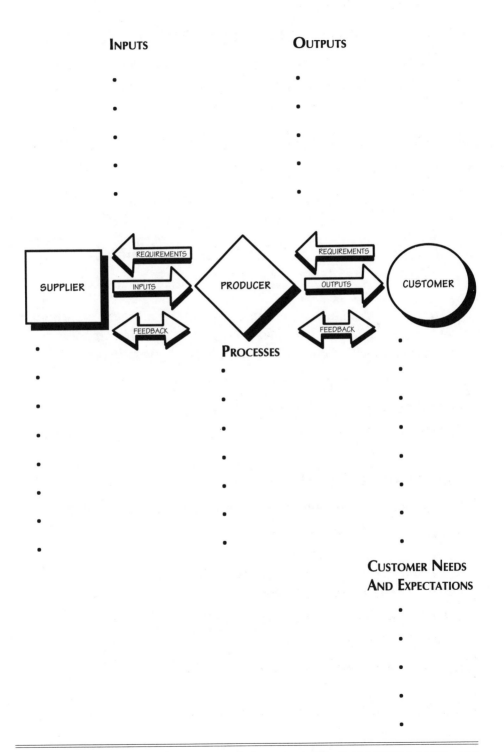

INPUTS

-
-
-
-
-

OUTPUTS

-
-
-
-
-

SUPPLIER

REQUIREMENTS

INPUTS

FEEDBACK

PRODUCER

REQUIREMENTS

OUTPUTS

FEEDBACK

CUSTOMER

PROCESSES

-
-
-
-
-
-
-
-

-
-
-
-
-
-

-
-
-
-
-
-
-
-

CUSTOMER NEEDS
AND EXPECTATIONS

-
-
-
-

NOMINAL GROUP TECHNIQUE

What Is The Nominal Group Technique?

The Nominal Group Technique *(NGT)* combines aspects of silent voting with limited discussion to help you build consensus and arrive at a team decision.

When Should The NGT Be Used?

Use the NGT when:

✍ Dealing with a sensitive, controversial, or prominent issue and you think contrary opinions and a myriad of details may paralyze the discussion. *(Using the NGT, the first round of ideas is generated silently, so discussion is held off until all ideas have been presented.)*

✍ You want to ensure equal participation by all team members. *(Using the NGT, each member has an equal opportunity to contribute, regardless of rank, seniority, or personality.)*

✍ A team has identified the root cause of a problem, but identifying a course of action from many alternatives is difficult.

The Seven Steps Of The NGT

Step 1: Define the problem to be solved or the decision to be made

Step 2: Silently generate ideas

Step 3: State and record ideas

Step 4: Clarify each item on the list

Step 5: Rank items silently; list rankings

Step 6: Tally rankings

Step 7: Wrap up the NGT session

Step 1: Define the problem to be solved or decision to be made

The problem, or decision, should be clearly defined and understood at the beginning of the session. Post a brief but complete statement outlining the problem/decision so all team members can read it.

Step 2: Silently generate ideas

Silently and independently, each team member writes down his or her ideas in a few words or a short phrase. The team can work within a five-minute time limit, or each member can try to come up with 10 or 12 ideas.

Step 3: State and record ideas

In round-robin fashion, team members should offer one idea from their lists. The Recorder simultaneously writes the ideas on a flip chart or board visible to the group. The round-robin process continues until each person has given all of his or her ideas. The Recorder should not duplicate items. If items are combined, the Recorder should make sure the team agrees that the ideas are, in fact, related. At this point, team members still don't discuss ideas; that comes in the next step.

During this phase, team members are encouraged to *"piggyback."* A person hitchhikes by thinking of a new idea after hearing another member's idea. Everyone is encouraged to add new ideas to the list and offer them on their next turn.

Step 4: Clarify each item on the list

For each item on the list from Step 3, allow an equal amount of time for group discussion. The objective here is to clarify each idea in case the wording is not clear, and not to win arguments. This step should be led by a group leader or facilitator. The leader reads each idea aloud, asks if there are any questions, and is responsible for keeping the group moving through the list.

Step 5: Rank items silently; list rankings

Assign a letter to each idea listed on the flip chart. For example, if you end up with six ideas, then you have statements labeled, "A, B, C, D, E, F."

Ask each team member to write down the letters corresponding to those listed on the flip chart.

Ask each team member to vote silently for the idea that best solves the problem or addresses the issue you are deciding. Assign a "1" to that idea. Assign a "2" to the second best idea, and so on. The higher the number, the less important the idea is to the individual who is silently voting.

As an alternative, if there is a long list of ideas to rank (*more than a dozen*) the team may use the "*half plus one*" rule. This rule suggests ranking only half of the items generated by the group, plus one. For example, if there were 30 items on the list, they would rank 16 of them in descending order of importance—from 1 to 16.

Step 6: Tally rankings

In this step, each team member calls out their rankings. The Recorder lists them on a flip chart. Add up each line of numbers horizontally. The item with the lowest total represents the team's decision up to this point—prior to discussion of the merits of the ideas.

Step 7: Wrap up the NGT session

List the items your team has agreed upon in descending order on a flip chart or board. Clarify again the definitions of the items. Discuss the vote openly. The purpose of the discussion is to find out if the final vote seems consistent and to reconsider items that may have received the wrong number (*too few or too many*) of votes. If things seem inconsistent, you might want to vote again.

Choose the next course of action and assign tasks to the appropriate team members. Thank everyone for their time, energy, ideas and cooperation.

KEY RESULT AREAS

KRA 1	
KRA 2	
KRA 3	
KRA 4	
KRA 5	
KRA 6	
KRA 7	
KRA 8	
KRA 9	

CRITERIA CHECK-OFF LIST

KRA:	CRITERIA QUESTION					
Potential KI	1	2	3	4	5	6

KI DATA COLLECTION WORKSHEET

KRAs/KIs	METHODS	TARGETS
KRA:		
KI 1:	Who: How: Where: When:	
KI 2:	Who: How: Where: When:	
KI 3:	Who: How: Where: When:	
KI 4:	Who: How: Where: When:	
KI 5:	Who: How: Where: When:	

KRA Tracking Matrix

Work Group: _____

Date: _____

KRA: _____

	1	2	3	4
KI				
Current Performance				

Common Performance Levels

				←	**10**	"Stretch"
				←	**9**	"Target"
				←	**8**	
				←	**7**	
				←	**6**	
				←	**5**	
				←	**4**	
				←	**3**	"Baseline"
				←	**2**	
				←	**1**	
				←	**0**	

Performance Level Score					**Index**
Weight					
Weighted Value					

THE PRACTICAL GUIDEBOOK COLLECTION FROM RICHARD CHANG ASSOCIATES, INC. PUBLICATIONS DIVISION

Our Practical Guidebook Collection is growing to meet the challenges of the ever-changing workplace of the 90's. Available through Richard Chang Associates, Inc., fine bookstores, training and organizational development resource catalogs and distributed internationally.

QUALITY IMPROVEMENT SERIES

- Meetings That Work!
- Continuous Improvement Tools Volume 1
- Continuous Improvement Tools Volume 2
- Step-By-Step Problem Solving
- Satisfying Internal Customers First!
- Continuous Process Improvement
- Improving Through Benchmarking
- Succeeding As A Self-Managed Team
- Process Reengineering In Action
- Measuring Organizational Improvement Impact

MANAGEMENT SKILLS SERIES

- Coaching Through Effective Feedback
- Expanding Leadership Impact
- Mastering Change Management
- On-The-Job Orientation And Training
- Re-Creating Teams During Transitions

HIGH PERFORMANCE TEAM SERIES

- Success Through Teamwork
- Team Decision-Making Techniques
- Measuring Team Performance
- Building A Dynamic Team

HIGH-IMPACT TRAINING SERIES

- Creating High-Impact Training
- Identifying Targeted Training Needs
- Mapping A Winning Training Approach
- Producing High-Impact Learning Tools
- Applying Successful Training Techniques
- Measuring The Impact Of Training
- Make Your Training Results Last

WORKPLACE DIVERSITY SERIES

- Capitalizing On Workplace Diversity
- Successful Staffing In A Diverse Workplace
- Team Building For Diverse Work Groups
- Communicating In A Diverse Workplace
- Tools For Valuing Diversity

ADDITIONAL RESOURCES
FROM RICHARD CHANG ASSOCIATES, INC.

Improve your training sessions and seminars with the ideal tools—videos from Richard Chang Associates, Inc. You and your team will easily relate to the portrayals of real-life workplace situations. You can apply our innovative techniques to your own situations for immediate results.

TRAINING VIDEOTAPES

Mastering Change Management*
Turning Obstacles Into Opportunities

Step-By-Step Problem Solving*
A Practical Approach To Solving Problems On The Job

Quality: You Don't Have To Be Sick To Get Better**
Individuals Do Make a Difference

Achieving Results Through Quality Improvement**

*Authored by Dr. Richard Chang and produced by Double Vision Studios.
**Produced by American Media Inc. in conjunction with Richard Chang Associates, Inc.
  Each video includes a Facilitator's Guide.

"THE HUMAN EDGE SERIES" VIDEOTAPES

Total Quality: Myths, Methods, Or Miracles
Featuring Drs. Ken Blanchard and Richard Chang

Empowering The Quality Effort
Featuring Drs. Ken Blanchard and Richard Chang

Produced by Double Vision Studios.

"THE TOTAL QUALITY SERIES"
TRAINING VIDEOTAPES AND WORKBOOKS

Building Commitment *(Telly Award Winner)*
How To Build Greater Commitment To Your TQ Efforts

Teaming Up
How To Successfully Participate On Quality-Improvement Teams

Applied Problem Solving
How To Solve Problems As An Individual Or On A Team

Self-Directed Evaluation
How To Establish Feedback Methods To Self-Monitor Improvements

Authored by Dr. Richard Chang and produced by Double Vision Studios, each videotape from *"The Total Quality Series"* includes a *Facilitator's Guide* and five *Participant Workbooks* with each purchase. Additional *Participant Workbooks* are available for purchase.

EVALUATION AND FEEDBACK FORM

We need your help to continuously improve the quality of the resources provided through the Richard Chang Associates, Inc., Publications Division. We would greatly appreciate your input and suggestions regarding this particular guidebook, as well as future guidebook interests.

Please photocopy this form before completing it, since other readers may use this guidebook. Thank you in advance for your feedback.

Guidebook Title: _____

1. Overall, how would you rate your *level of satisfaction* with this guidebook? Please circle your response.

   Extremely Dissatisfied   Satisfied   Extremely Satisfied

   1   2   3   4   5

2. What specific *concepts or methods* did you find <u>most</u> helpful?

   _____
   _____

3. What specific *concepts or methods* did you find <u>least</u> helpful?

   _____
   _____

4. As an individual who may purchase additional guidebooks in the future, what *characteristics/features/benefits* are most important to you in making a decision to purchase a guidebook *(or another similar book)*?

   _____
   _____

5. What additional *subject matter/topic areas* would you like to see addressed in future guidebooks?

   _____
   _____

Name *(optional):*_____

Address: _____

C/S/Z: _____   **Phone (   )** _____

PLEASE FAX YOUR RESPONSES TO: (714) 756-0853
OR CALL US AT: 1-800-756-8096